Plantation Kingdom

The Marcus Cunliffe Lecture Series

RICHARD FOLLETT, SERIES EDITOR

Plantation Kingdom

The American South and Its Global Commodities

RICHARD FOLLETT
SVEN BECKERT
PETER COCLANIS
BARBARA HAHN

Johns Hopkins University Press
Baltimore

Johns Hopkins University Press
2715 North Charles Street
Baltimore, Maryland 21218-4363
www.press.jhu.edu

Library of Congress Cataloging-in-Publication Data

Names: Follett, Richard, 1968– author. | Beckert, Sven, author. |
Coclanis, Peter, 1952– author. | Hahn, Barbara, 1967– author.
Title: Plantation kingdom : the American South and its global commodities /
by Richard Follett, Sven Beckert, Peter Coclanis, and Barbara Hahn.
Description: Baltimore : Johns Hopkins University Press, [2016] | Series: The
Marcus Cunliffe lecture series | Includes bibliographical references and index.
Identifiers: LCCN 2015026982| ISBN 9781421419398 (hardcover : alkaline paper)
| ISBN 9781421419404 (paperback : alkaline paper) | ISBN 9781421419411
(electronic) | ISBN 1421419394 (hardcover : alkaline paper) | ISBN
1421419408 (paperback : alkaline paper) | ISBN 1421419416 (electronic)
Subjects: LCSH: Southern States—Economic conditions. | Plantations—Economic
aspects—Southern States—History. | Agriculture—Economic
aspects—Southern States—History. | Tobacco industry—Southern
States—History. | Rice trade—Southern States—History. | Sugar
trade—Southern States—History. | Cotton trade—Southern States—History.
| Slavery—Economic aspects—Southern States—History. | African
Americans—Southern States—Economic conditions. | Slaves—United
States—Social conditions.
Classification: LCC HC107.A13 F67 2016 | DDC 382/.410975—dc23 LC record available at
http://lccn.loc.gov/2015026982

A catalog record for this book is available from the British Library.

*Special discounts are available for bulk purchases of this book. For more information, please
contact Special Sales at 410-516-6936 or specialsales@press.jhu.edu.*

Johns Hopkins University Press uses environmentally friendly book
materials, including recycled text paper that is composed of at least 30 percent
post-consumer waste, whenever possible.

CONTENTS

❦

Introduction   1
RICHARD FOLLETT

The Road to Commodity Hell:
The Rise and Fall of the First American Rice Industry   12
PETER A. COCLANIS

Cotton and the US South: A Short History   39
SVEN BECKERT

The Rise and Fall of American Sugar   61
RICHARD FOLLETT

Tobacco's Commodity Route   91
BARBARA HAHN

Conclusion   119
RICHARD FOLLETT

Notes   123
Guide to Further Reading   151
Index   159

Plantation Kingdom

RICHARD FOLLETT

Introduction

❧

"**COTTON IS KING,**" blasted South Carolinian James Henry Hammond on the floor of the US Senate in 1858. "Who can doubt that cotton is supreme?" the rambunctious Southerner declared. "You dare not make war against it." By his estimates alone, the South's four principal plantation crops—cotton, rice, sugar, and tobacco—generated wealth and exports that enriched the nation. He was right: the Southern states produced three-quarters of all cotton consumed by Britain, Europe, and the rest of the United States. With land aplenty, "the finest soil, and the most delightful climate," Hammond asked whether the American South had "territory enough to make an empire that shall rule the world." The great valley of the Mississippi, the South Carolinian announced, was the "acknowledged seat" of the South's commercial empire, and its sway "will be as great as ever the Nile knew in the earlier ages of mankind."[1]

Hammond's empire unraveled in the bloody battle fields of the American Civil War. Confederate soldiers and generations of Americans, however, never forgot the centrality of export commodities to the Southern experience. "Dixie," the unacknowledged anthem of the Confederate States of America, did not pull its punches. "In the Land of Cotton," the famous ballad went, "Old Times they are not forgotten." Old times were hard times too, for the Southern agricultural empire echoed to the sounds of whips, chains, and work bells. Almost four million enslaved African Americans toiled in Dixie's land, winnowing rice in disease-infested swamps, cultivating fields of cotton from the Carolinas to Texas, cutting sugar cane along the banks of the Mississippi, or picking tobacco leaves in the lands made rich by slaveholders in the seventeenth century. The Civil War and emancipation mercifully abolished racial slavery, bringing to an end a violent system of enforced, bonded labor upon which the New World plantation system rested. Countless audiences, however, sought to remember differently. As David O. Selznick unforgettably reminded moviegoers in 1939, the Old South was a "Land of Cavaliers and Cotton Fields. . . . Look for it only in books," the Hollywood producer announced, "for it is no more than a dream remembered, a civilization gone with the wind."[2]

This book tells the story of the rise and the fall of America's plantation kingdom. It explains how and why Americans began to cultivate the four great staple crops of Southern life; it considers the fundamental—determinative—role of enslaved and forced labor in the emergence, maintenance, and decline of America's plantation staples, and it traces the efforts of rapacious entrepreneurs to reshape the Southern landscape in the name of profit and productivity. Readers keen to find cavaliers and moonlit dreams, however, will be sorely disappointed. In their place are the real Americans, free and unfree, who transformed the countryside and produced the raw materials from which much of the nation's wealth derived. Land-hungry colonial Virginians take their place alongside hardscrabble farmers who uprooted trees and broke the sod on the cotton frontier. Shoulder to shoulder with these agricultural capitalists stand eighteenth-century tycoons—who amassed vast personal fortunes from rice lands—and nineteenth-century sugar lords who stood atop America's most industrialized, capital-intensive plantation regime. Although some were fabulously rich, these men and women were members of an aspiring farming and plantation class, and their chief motivations lay in wealth and power. Slavery, however, sharply distinguished the Old South from the rest of the country—racial bondage, not free market relations, dictated antebellum labor markets; labor-intensive production techniques endured; vast armies of enslaved workers toiled from sunup to sundown in work gangs; and the raw power that slaveholders exercised unleashed a violent, repressive world where planters' wealth derived in no small measure from the sweated labor of their enslaved property. Slaveholders entertained no guilt over slavery. For them, racial slavery provided a steady, albeit sometimes refractory, workforce; it offered the only recognizable source of massed gang laborers for large-scale plantation agriculture, and slavery offered a tried and tested route to wealth accumulation.

No man is an island, however, and no kingdom lasts forever. As this short book makes clear, American farmers were thoroughly embedded in world export markets where competition proved fierce and where federal and state governments proved a valued, if sometimes fickle and occasionally disruptive, friend. By the eve of the First World War, when this book comes to a close, the once proud, indomitable plantation kingdom lay in tatters. American cotton no longer held sway in world cotton markets, US tobacco growers worked to the drumbeat of powerful Northern and transnational trusts, Carolina's rice fields dried up only to be replaced by golf courses and luxury condos in the 1950s, and the once rich sugar magnates of the Mississippi valley sold out or hung on for dear life, desperate for federal subsidies or tariff protection. Cotton growers in India spun thread more cheaply than any American farmer could manage, rice cultivators throughout Southeast Asia made Georgia and South Carolina's production irrelevant, European sugar beets and duty-free sugar cane knocked America's domestic sugar cane industry sideways, and cheaper tobacco strains ensured that global competition burrowed its way into the heart of Kentucky's so-called Black Patch.

Global competition is, of course, axiomatic to the modern world. We live in an era of global interconnectedness where local and international forces coexist, sometimes uneasily, occasionally in harmony. Even this book is testament to international collaboration. The four contributors—two Europeans and two Americans—are leading experts in the histories of cotton, sugar, rice, and tobacco. They have published on many aspects of eighteenth- and nineteenth-century

American history and authored several of the principal texts on America's plantation crops. They gathered at the University of Sussex in Brighton, England, to deliver the Marcus Cunliffe lectures on the American South and its global commodities in 2012 and 2013. The essays reveal a number of core themes. First, like this book, Southern themes proved to be international in scale and scope. Indeed, the global movement of labor and export commodities lay at the axis of New World slavery, and, as Peter Coclanis indicates in his chapter on the rise and subsequent collapse of the American rice industry, South Carolinian planter-entrepreneurs proved singularly adept at amassing capital, wealth, and enslaved workers. Commodifying land and labor, slaveholders oversaw a plantation revolution along the Carolina shore. By the early 1710s, the enslaved population surpassed its white equivalent. Some of the newly enslaved came from the rice-growing regions of Senegambia and may possibly have introduced aspects of African risiculture to the Carolinas. By 1740, however, almost forty thousand African and African American slaves resided in the colony, and the workforce was thoroughly Africanized, with two out of every three slaves born in Africa. Rice exports similarly surged forward, rising from less than three hundred thousand pounds per annum in the late 1690s to thirty million pounds in 1740. Charleston served as the nerve center of a new plantation economy that pulsed with the availability of capital and enslaved labor. As Coclanis points out, the wealth derived from the international rice trade beggars belief. By the 1770s, free Charlestonians were considerably better off than their compatriots elsewhere in British North America, and this trend continued as late as the Civil War. Carolinians, moreover, dominated eighteenth-century rice markets, albeit in the Western economies, and they traded their commodity with method and rigor.[3]

If North American rice served as a leitmotif of early international trade success, US cotton planters enjoyed phenomenal gains from their privileged position as the globe's premier cotton supplier in the nineteenth century. Sven Beckert indicates just how deeply international cotton markets penetrated the lives of free and enslaved Americans. America's dominance rested on the cultivation of short-staple, upland cotton. Eli Whitney's cotton gin broke the technological bottleneck to enhanced production, and, from the 1810s, the promise of good profits lured generations of settlers to the western cotton fields. Credit poured into the cotton states from British, French, and Northern bankers, ensuring that an international boom in cotton demand translated into a feverish thirst for land and labor. Slave capital alone represented 45.8 percent of the total wealth of the cotton-producing states in 1860. Indeed, cotton and slaveholding were widespread and deeply entrenched throughout the slave states. By the time James Henry Hammond gave his stalwart defense of King Cotton, US growers stood atop a globally integrated market where Southern cotton and British finance zipped back and forth across the Atlantic, enriching merchants, bankers, insurance agents, and industrialists from Liverpool to Lowell.[4]

A decade later and following the bloodiest emancipation process of all New World slave societies—unlike the gradualist and compensated abolition programs of the Caribbean and Latin America, slave emancipation in the United States advanced by force of arms and military defeat of the world's most powerful slaveholding class—America's plantation kingdom lay in ruin, its slaves emancipated and its once powerful slaveholders bankrupted. Defeated Southern planters received not a penny in compensation for their erstwhile slave property, and, for their part, freedpeople secured no land in the postwar Reconstruction settlement. Emancipation quickly proved to be America's "unfinished revolution," but, for those who still resided in the plantation mansions, the economic dislocation was without parallel. Indeed, as one historian observed, the most apt comparison to the South's postwar economic contraction might be Russia after the 1917 revolution. There, Lenin's Communists outlawed income-producing private property. Lincoln's disciples were hardly Communists, but in the half century between America's Civil War and the Russian Revolution, Southern agriculture swiftly descended into what Coclanis calls "commodity hell." In rice, cotton, sugar, and tobacco markets, US goods competed against cheaply produced and almost identical foreign (and sometimes domestic) commodities. Whatever natural advantage Southern producers once enjoyed, by the last quarter of the nineteenth century, they faced undifferentiated markets, global and imperial rivalries, free trade, and the uncertainties of transnational commerce. Frequently undercut or outproduced by offshore competitors, American planters struggled to maintain their market share, let alone their once-prominent status. The road to perdition was steep and calamitous. At the foot of the Mississippi, New Orleans' merchants felt the cold winds blow soon after the Civil War. Cotton receipts in the city plummeted, and prewar wealth evaporated with slave emancipation. Louisiana fell precipitously from second to thirty-seventh in the nation in per capita wealth. America's sugar cane industry drowned in global competition. As Richard Follett demonstrates, US cane growers had long struggled to wring sustained profits from their sugar lands, but, with the arrival of duty-free imported sugars, the death knell sounded over the region's cane industry.[5]

For many years, historians fiercely crossed swords over the nature of the nineteenth-century South, asking, What was exceptional or not about the Southern states; did the region converge or diverge from national norms; did slavery halt, hinder, or advance capitalism (and if so in what ways); did liberal values trump slaveholders' reticence over market relations; and what were the peculiar legacies of slavery (and its social and economic relations of production) on the region's history? Many of those questions remain contested among historians, though the polarization that once characterized the slavery debates in the 1970s and 1980s has now given way to a scholarly consensus: pre-industrial relations of production (unwaged slavery) coexisted with acquisitive market values, particularly during the nineteenth century when slave-based agriculture posted unprecedented profits. So explosive and dynamic was America's plantation complex that some scholars now place slavery at the cornerstone of a new history of American capitalism.[6]

Each chapter in this book examines the history of a specific commodity, tracing its consumption, markets, and the degree to which capitalism determined social and economic relations. Whether in rice, cotton, sugar, or tobacco, Southern planters and their enslaved workforce transformed landscapes, invested in relevant technology (particularly in the sugar cane industry), amassed land, and emptied their pocketbooks for yet more slaves. Southern slaveholders did not shy from the opportunities at hand. They recognized, like Karl Marx, that "the price paid for a slave is nothing but the anticipated and capitalized surplus-value or profit to be wrung out of the slave." And wrung they surely were. Enslaved people shaped the Mississippi valley, they cleared tens of thousands of acres, barricading them behind mile after mile of earthen levees, and they grew cotton in vast, unheard-of quantities. Irrespective of the human suffering—among the enslaved who bore the brunt of the plantation revolution—the results were spectacular. On the western edge of the American cotton empire, one settler along Louisiana's Red River gushed, "I had heard of the immense cotton fields that grow in this country but they never gave me an idea. . . . [W]hen I beheld the cotton I was perfectly amazed."[7]

The rapid transformation of the Southern countryside, and its integration within national and international markets, unleashed monumental, even amazing change. This nineteenth-century phenomenon—called "second slavery" by some historians—was distinct from the colonial regime in that new commodities, raised in unprecedented quantities, triumphed in regions that had been thus far marginal to the Atlantic economy. At the heart of this nineteenth-century transformation was the systematic expansion of Atlantic slavery, the mass concentration of slave labor devoted to staple crop production, the development of new geographical regions to supply slave-grown plantation commodities to expanding world markets, and the use of land and labor on a new industrial scale.[8]

Throughout the South, aspects of this second slavery occurred. Antebellum cotton farming spread west and labor productivity rose, while markets for enslaved and agricultural commodities expanded in unprecedented ways. Along the banks of the Mississippi, Delta cotton and Louisiana sugar rose triumphant, but the old southwestern states were not alone in being swept up in the plantation revolution. As Barbara Hahn indicates in her chapter on tobacco, over the course of the eighteenth and nineteenth centuries, the locus of production shifted from the coastal Chesapeake to the tobacco fields of North Carolina's piedmont and the rich tobacco-growing soils of western Kentucky. By exploring the workings of the market economy in tobacco—the oldest of the Southern plantation crops—Hahn demonstrates the range and diversity of crop production systems, technical innovations, and the adaptive responses planters embraced to maximize yields of particularly desirable tobacco leaves. Like others who have recently considered the dynamism and creativity of American agricultural development, Hahn's analysis stresses how consumer and market choices interacted with cultivation practices and production techniques. Tobacco farming, moreover, evolved within the particular dynamics of colonial and national politics. As Hahn makes clear, not only did Britain's attempts to regulate the tobacco market shape the types of tobacco grown in colonial Virginia but foreign demand for particular types of sweet or bitter tobacco continued to influence tobacco growers late into the nineteenth century. Market forces and new regulatory frameworks introduced by successive US governments encouraged tobacco farmers to adopt specific plant varietals and cultivation techniques, but so too did the rapid emergence of the cigarette industry, as discussed toward the close of Hahn's essay. Whether badgered by British legislation in the 1670s or by the American tobacco trust two hundred years later, tobacco farmers nevertheless attempted to exercise some leverage over farm production, irrespective of the powerful imperial and global dimensions to their trade.[9]

Like the region's tobacco farmers, staple-crop producers across the South faced an uneasy relationship with the modern state. Cotton growers, Sven Beckert indicates, had every reason to cheer the nation's rapid geographic expansion. The forced removal of indigenous peoples from rich cotton-growing soils, the acquisition of the vast Louisiana Territory in 1803, and the military conquest of America's Southwest enabled planters to spread their peculiar brand of Southern slave-based capitalism across the continent. The rise of political antislavery, however, challenged Southerners' allegiances to the Union, which finally snapped in the winter and spring of 1861. For their part, American sugar planters did not (at least initially) wish to leave the Union. Federal tariffs provided a lifeline to a cane sugar industry that had grown rapidly during the previous fifty years but that already faced stiff international competition even in a relatively protected market. Richard Follett unpacks the shifting and frequently unhappy relationships among domestic sugar cane planters, foreign competition, tariff legislation, and the US state. As his chapter reminds us, labor supply—and the maintenance of forced labor—proved central to the US cane sugar industry. Emancipation unleashed colossal change in America's cane world, eliminating without compensation $100 million of private capital from the portfolios of the sugar elite and abolishing the forced dominion of master over slave. No longer labor lords with their wealth concentrated in moveable assets (enslaved people), sugar farmers redoubled their commitment to land as the primary form of wealth holding and to cheap labor as a principal determinant in production and profitability. Indeed, like sugar planters elsewhere, America's cane lords attempted to maintain the plantation system by contracting laborers from low-income nations, specifically China. In other tropical cane economies, the expansive European nation-states facilitated the new traffic in humans but the labor experiments in Louisiana (where the vast majority of US domestic sugar was manufactured) faltered and failed to supplant the domestic and overwhelmingly African American population from the sugar fields. Unlike their enslaved predecessors, cane workers received payment for their labor, though coercion remained pivotal to the maintenance of the plantation mode of production.[10]

As Follett demonstrates, a process of consolidation and rationalization ultimately brought the sugar plantation system to an end. A small number of sugar factories replaced hundreds of independent stand-alone plantation mills and sugar-producing facilities. Foreign capital and corporate cooperatives muscled into the sugar industry, but America's domestic producers could not withstand the onslaught of global competition once the United States acquired a tropical empire of its own. The introduction of Hawaiian, Puerto Rican, Cuban, and Philippine sugar at duty-free or substantially reduced rates delivered the hammer blow to Louisiana's cane interests. The availability of cheaply produced beet sugar was the sucker punch from which America's once rich cane sugar kingdom never recovered.

The plantation system, upon which New World rice, cotton, sugar, and tobacco rested for three centuries, came fitfully to a close. Vast estates, of course, continued to exist, but the estate-based plantation order was gradually replaced by tenancy and sharecropping across much of the rural South. Poverty and forced labor endured, however, haunting the region well into the twentieth century. Trapped in the vice-like grip of debt peonage, African American sharecroppers encountered their own commodity hell. Tied to the soil and in perpetual debt to landlords, the sons, daughters, and grandchildren of America's enslaved millions limped into the twentieth century mired in semifeudal relations with the descendants of Dixie's slaveholding elite.[11]

This book brings together in a short, concise volume four interlocking and interrelated essays. It does not address every crop grown on plantations. Hemp and corn are excluded; the value of the former remained small, and although corn was grown abundantly—it was by far the leading Southern crop by acreage—its value did not register very much in markets, particularly global markets. By contrast, each essay in *Plantation Kingdom* examines one of the four principal export crops produced in the American South over the eighteenth and nineteenth centuries. Each case study provides a slightly different perspective. Coclanis looks at demand and supply—the basis by which any capitalist economy ticks. Beckert argues that the American South and its cotton complex served as a "giant laboratory of global capitalism." Follett explores the place of American sugar producers in a world economy and contends that Louisiana was the last of the New World sugar colonies, whose rise and fall followed the contours of other cane societies around the world. Hahn demonstrates the imperiled position of American tobacco farmers, who navigated imperial and global markets, altering production and developing new varietals to meet the burgeoning demand. Whatever the crop or commodity, the story told in this book delivers powerfully familiar lessons. Dixie did not prove quite as bulletproof as James Henry Hammond predicted in 1858. King Cotton fell from grace, the Mississippi never reached the greatness of the Pharaoh's Nile, and New Orleans—the once regal entrepôt of Southern trade—found itself dethroned by global competition. As we in the Western economies know only too well, nations rise and fall, new and developing economies emerge, global capital and trade moves to wherever production costs are cheapest, and once powerful economic kingdoms wither on the vine. Nowhere were those startlingly familiar themes exposed more clearly than in the rise and fall of America's plantation complex.

PETER A. COCLANIS

The Road to Commodity Hell

❧

The Rise and Fall of the First American Rice Industry

FROM THE SOUTH'S earliest beginnings, tobacco, cotton, sugar, rice, and the enslaved people who raised those crops were bought and sold, traded and mortgaged as commodities. As John Locke, a salient figure in the early history of Carolina, the epicenter of the Southern rice industry for much of its history, put it in the seventeenth century, "Commodities are Moveables, valuable by Money, the common measure."[1] By that reckoning, the two "Moveables, valuable by money," that are central to this chapter—rice and slaves—originated thousands of miles from the American South, and, like the other slave-grown products described in this book, they were shipped and sold as marketable commodities throughout the Atlantic world.

It is not easy to define the term *commodity* even when restricted to economics. Used generically, the term refers to any marketable item—whether tangible good or service—of material value. Although the term, used in this way in English, dates back to circa 1400 CE, it has over time increasingly taken on a more specific meaning, namely, a class or type of marketable good or service, members of which are generally sold in a rather undifferentiated, interchangeable manner and which at one end of the spectrum possess complete fungibility.[2] Totally fungible goods such as gold comprise individual units that are—or can be made—mutually substitutable with one another. In other words, an ounce of gold is an ounce of gold, whether it exists in the form of a bar, a coin, or a bracelet. Ten dollars is ten dollars whether consisting of one $10 bill, two $5 bills, or ten $1 bills.

Few goods or services are sold totally without differentiation (or attention to particular target markets), but goods or services marketed as commodities are sufficiently standardized—generic, as it were—that no one cares much where they come from or who supplies them. As Marx, referring to wheat, famously put it in 1859 in *The Critique of Political Economy*, "From the taste of wheat it is not possible to tell who produced it, a Russian serf, a French peasant or an English capitalist."[3] Standardized, even homogenized, wheat had largely become a commodity in the West.

By the time that Marx wrote, rice was a long-established commodity in Asia—indeed, the world's first functional commodity futures market was established in 1730 at the Dōjima Rice Exchange in Osaka, Japan—but this particular cereal grain was still in the process of becoming a commodity in the West.[4] Southern US producers, as this chapter unveils, fought the commodification process for a long time, albeit ultimately unsuccessfully. In the late nineteenth century, Southern producers—at least those in the South Atlantic states—experienced economic pain and even punishment. Once exalted as grandees who lorded over the so-called low country of South Carolina and Georgia, the region's rice magnates now faced crowded markets, interchangeable products, and vigorous global competition. In short, they faced a condition familiar to the trade literature today, "commodity hell," and with it a century of economic perdition as well.

Rice Consumption

Rice differs substantially, even dramatically, from the other crops treated in this book. Unlike cotton, tobacco, and sugar, it is a basic foodstuff, indeed, according to many the most important cereal grain in the world. Nor is that the only difference between rice and the other crops being featured. While rice historically has been grown for domestic consumption in a number of places around the Atlantic world, it was central to the development of only a few: scattered places in

West Africa, northwestern Italy, a few areas in Spain, parts of Brazil, the southeastern coast of North America, and, beginning around the time the story told here ends, in southwestern Louisiana and southeast Texas, followed shortly thereafter by east central Arkansas and, then, the Sacramento Valley of California.[5]

Consumption patterns in the West differentiate rice from these other commodities as well. Whereas demand for cotton, tobacco, and sugar is relatively straightforward and the markets for each relatively easy to trace, demand for rice is rather mysterious, as the cereal, for better or worse, is a minor product in the West. Moreover, whereas sugar alone was sufficiently important to explain a great deal about the workings of the Atlantic economy in the seventeenth and eighteenth centuries and cotton sufficiently important to do the same for the nineteenth, rice in and of itself explains little about this Atlantic economy as a whole. To be sure, rice had many uses in the West—but they were often intermediate, if not invisible—which makes the rice market difficult to generalize about or to document fully or, at times, to trace. Thus, if rice has dominated the lives of populations in much of Asia over the millennia, in the West it has impacted relatively few, and its market power has never been determinative.[6]

The place of rice has always been particularly enigmatic in the United States. Today, for example, the United States is a major rice producer and one of the top exporting nations in the world, but per capita rice consumption is very low. Americans get about 3 percent of their calories from rice, as opposed to 16–17 percent from added sugar alone. There are few producers, and many, if not most, Americans are almost completely unaware that there even is a US rice industry.[7] Even in history, the story of rice in the United States—whether we are talking about the ideology and political views of the planters, the culture of the labor force, or the industry's characteristic work rhythms and routines—has often seemed a bit out of step, off kilter, aberrant, at times even extreme. One unfortunate result of such framing has been a tendency to exaggerate, romanticize, or exoticize the behavior and worldviews of those involved in the industry, positioning rice in another world, if not a parallel universe, far, far out of the mainstream.

In light of the above qualifications, why bother at all to study rice in the Atlantic world? The most significant reason is that the evolution of the industry provides important insights into the expansion and elaboration of global capitalism and the positive and negative factors relating to it. The process by which rice from the United States became commodified is a similarly revealing one, and the fact that rice—unlike cotton, tobacco, or sugar—is both a basic foodstuff and an export commodity allows us to compare and contrast its trajectory with those very different kinds of agricultural products.

Origins of Rice Cultivation

In comparison to Afro-Eurasia, rice cultivation in the Western Hemisphere does not have deep roots. Most specialists believe that rice (*Oryza sativa*) was first domesticated in southern China roughly twelve thousand years ago, whence it spread through other parts of Asia and, later, to Africa and Europe. *Oryza sativa* has always been by far the most prevalent species of rice cultivated in the world, though it should be noted that domestication of a second important species, *Oryza glaberrima*, began in West Africa two to three thousand years ago. Both of these species crossed the Atlantic with Europeans and Africans as part of what many refer to as the Columbian exchange beginning in the late fifteenth century. Although both established themselves as cultivars in the New World, *O. sativa* was grown much more widely, and it alone was commercialized. That said, over the centuries small amounts of *O. glaberrima* were grown for home consumption by African and African American populations in parts of the Americas.[8]

Contrary to conventional wisdom, or at least common belief, rice does not have to be produced in paddies in hot, humid climates. The plant is actually quite adaptable and historically has been cultivated in a wide range of latitudes and at various elevations. Water and sun are essential—the sine qua nons—for rice cultivation, not conical hats and water buffaloes. Indeed, rice (like the other commodities in this book) is grown in significant quantities today in highly diverse agroclimates in areas ranging from Australia to Egypt, from Spain to Korea, and from Missouri to Vietnam. In the Western Hemisphere during the early modern period, rice cultivation was attempted in places ranging from the central Andes to Virginia. It took hold early on in northeastern Brazil and in the circum-Caribbean basin, where it was grown in small quantities, generally for home consumption. Rice grown in the Western Hemisphere did not "express" itself on export markets in a significant way until the early eighteenth century, when an export complex began to emerge in the English/British colony of South Carolina along the South Atlantic seaboard of North America. The ambiguous verb *express* is used here because its medical connotation—to manifest or produce symptoms—portends the way the rice industry in this area would later sicken and die. Another medical term—*iatrogenesis*, or complications arising inadvertently from medical treatment—is also an apt metaphor for analyzing the rise and fall of the South Atlantic rice industry, for the heavy reliance on exports that was responsible for the region's rise later proved its undoing.[9]

Some rice was grown in South Carolina from the first decade of settlement in the 1670s, but a rice industry (rudimentary though it was) did not emerge in the colony until the first third of the eighteenth century. Not until then were the minimal conditions necessary and sufficient for commercial rice production in place: a dependable and affordable agricultural labor force, some portion of which had experience in risiculture; adequate sources and stocks of physical and circulating capital; functional transportation and marketing infrastructure, networks, and channels; and requisite amounts of entrepreneurship and local knowledge.[10]

If the origins of rice cultivation in South Carolina are controversial—some, but no means all, scholars now accord enslaved Africans primary responsibility for introducing rice and rice technology to the New World—the manner in which commercial, export-oriented rice production in South Carolina came about is quite clear. No one doubts that the staple complex—based on the plantation production of rice, mostly for export, by enslaved Africans and African Americans—was the work of aggressive Euro-American and European agriculturalists, merchants, and financiers. Those merchant-capitalists vividly embodied the concept of entrepreneurship as it was developing in the eighteenth century, notably the risk-bearing function emphasized by Richard Cantillon, the Irish banker, who is seen as the first systematic theorist of entrepreneurship. Indeed, rice production in South Carolina, for a slew of reasons, was among the riskier business propositions at the time, particularly for those involved on the ground.[11]

One of the reasons that the origins of rice cultivation in South Carolina are so controversial is that documentary evidence and material remains are both scanty and murky. Many scholars believe that rice in the colony was first grown in small plots "dry"—without the benefit of irrigation facilities—on nonswamp ("high") lands in the eastern part of the colony. It became apparent relatively soon, however, that rice grew best on irrigated swampland, and the vast majority of rice was grown in such areas throughout the history of commercial production in South Carolina. The commercial rice zone in South Carolina was always centered in the low country, the easternmost third of the colony/state, first in scattered, freshwater ("inland") swamps and later in tidal swamps. In the former areas, swamps were drained, and rice was planted on the drained sites. Planters constructed rudimentary irrigation works nearby—water impoundments of one type or another generally—both to ensure adequate supplies of water at appropriate times in the growing season and to drain off excess water when necessary. Production in such irrigated swamps brought a greater degree of system, method, and coordination to cultivation—thereby reducing risk—but planters were still too dependent on rainfall and elementary water-capture technologies to suit their needs. As a result, inland swamps—sites of almost all of the rice grown in South Carolina in the first half of the eighteenth century—were increasingly displaced as production centers in the second half of that century by drained tidal swamplands in other parts of the low country where more sophisticated irrigation technology, closer calibration of production, and greater labor coordination could be employed. These swamps, generally closer to the coast, were located in narrow, geographically limited zones on or adjacent to South Carolina's principal tidal rivers.[12]

The tidal rice zone of South Carolina—along with later extensions in other parts of the South Atlantic coast ranging from the Cape Fear River in southeastern North Carolina in the north to the St. Johns River in northeastern Florida in the south—seems small, even puny compared to the major Asian rice-production zones such as the lower Yangtze Delta, the Ganges-Brahmaputra Delta, the Irrawaddy Delta, the alluvial plains of the Chao Phraya, or the Mekong Delta. Indeed, the amount of land devoted to rice cultivation along the South Atlantic coast of North America—even at its productive peak in the mid-nineteenth century—never comprised more than about 160,000–170,000 acres, numbers that would be considered no more than small rounding errors in an Asian context where the amount of land in production at the same time was at least five hundred times greater.[13]

Unlike short-staple cotton—the frontier for which seemed almost limitless in the American South in the early nineteenth century—though like Louisiana's spatially limited sugar industry (topics that will be addressed in subsequent chapters), rice cultivated via tidal action faced severe geographical and hydrological constraints from the start. The entrepreneurial decision to reposition South Carolinian rice cultivation in tidal zones was predicated on the idea that harnessing river tides to draw water onto and off diked fields would allow for greater water regulation and irrigation efficiency. Moreover, because weeds could be better controlled in tidal swaps, planters could reduce labor inputs during the growing season. Tidal cultivation did in fact work as intended—productivity was higher than in inland swamps—but the siting decision made for some serious problems nonetheless. First, the area where this system of production could operate, as indicated above, was very limited. Fields had to be located along stretches of low country rivers where the tidal action was strong enough to raise and lower water levels efficiently and consistently without getting too close to estuarial zones, where the water was too brackish to grow rice. After several decades—as well as significant discovery costs and considerable experimentation—rice planters and those who helped to finance their operations found that these conditions were generally met in river bands running between about ten and twenty miles from the coast. It was in such areas that the South Carolina rice industry was based, from the second half of the eighteenth century until its total collapse in the early twentieth century. In South Carolina, production centered along five tidal rivers: from northeast to southwest, the Santee, the Cooper, the Ashley, the Combahee, and the Savannah, the last of which constituted the border between South Carolina and Georgia. As time passed, commercial rice production spread to tidal rivers in other parts of the South Atlantic region. In addition to the Cape Fear River in southeastern North Carolina and the St. Johns River in northeastern Florida, five rivers in Georgia, which along with North Carolina began producing rice in commercial quantities in the 1750s, ultimately became sites of large-scale rice production: the Savannah, the Ogeechee, the Altamaha, the Satilla, and the St. Marys. For all intents and purposes, these rivers constituted the universe for commercial rice production in the South Atlantic colonies/states.[14]

In addition to the geographical and hydrological constraints outlined above, tidal cultivation exacerbated already profound epidemiological challenges, and—as discussed below—this underpinned and reinforced other factors working to "lock in" racial slavery as the dominant labor system in rice country. Given the fact that "wet" rice production imposed heavy labor requirements upon workers and that the tidal swamps were rife with mosquitos transmitting a variety of diseases (malaria, most notably), morbidity (disease incidence) and mortality (death) levels in the rice zone were extraordinarily high. Although they too suffered in this lethal environment, Africans and African Americans possessed higher degrees of inherited and acquired immunities to some of these mosquito-borne diseases, especially malaria. The arduous work regimen in rice, the epidemiological advantage possessed by Africans and African Americans, and prior experience and expertise in rice cultivation of at least some available Africans made African and African American workers the preferred option in rice cultivation.

That African and African American workers were subjected to slavery, the tightest and most coercive form of labor control of the era, was in part a function of the widespread acceptance of this labor institution among the European and Euro-American populations of the rice region. Of equal importance, it was simply impossible to induce or attract a sufficient number of free laborers to produce rice profitably on a large scale in this lethal environment. The above conditions go a long way toward explaining why Africans and African Americans, working as slaves until the Civil War and as free—or more accurately quasifree—laborers thereafter constituted the heart of the labor force in the South Atlantic rice industry throughout its history.[15]

The Rice Country's Elite

For those who financed and rendered operational the tidal rice regime, the profits were exhilarating. Although the fixed and variable capital costs entailed in establishing and maintaining rice works in the tidal zone were quite substantial, planters benefited from scale economies with large, heavily capitalized agricultural units worked by sizable numbers of enslaved laborers. Robust external demand for rice during the low country's rise to economic power in the second half of the eighteenth century created conditions necessary not only to establish and sustain the plantation rice complex of the South Atlantic region but to render the complex extraordinarily profitable— net rates of return were estimated at 25 percent annually at the time— and its leaders, the wealthiest planter class in North America for several generations. Alice Hanson Jones's foundational findings on wealth in British North America on the eve of the American Revolution demonstrate the rice planters' wealth in dramatic ways. According to Jones, in 1774 mean total wealth (per free capita) in the Charleston District—the epicenter of tidal rice country—was eleven times greater than the average for New England and nine times greater than the average for the Middle Colonies. Indeed, the figures for the Charleston District far outpace those for any other subregion in Jones's sample: the average for the second-wealthiest subregion—tobacco-growing Anne Arundel County, Maryland, where slavery was also prominent— was less than 30 percent of the figure for the Charleston District.[16]

Although its lead over the precociously industrializing Northeast was reduced in relative terms in the first half of the nineteenth century, the free population in the South Atlantic rice region remained extremely well off (on average) right down to the Civil War, far wealthier (on average) than populations anywhere in the North. In the South Carolina low country, for example, mean wealth per free capita in 1860 was $2253.60 (1860 dollars), while the corresponding figure for Massachusetts was $625.19, for New York $596.99, and for Pennsylvania $570.92. A small number of plantation districts in Mississippi, Alabama, and Louisiana's sugar country rivaled—and surpassed—the South Atlantic rice district in wealth per free capita by 1860, but, clearly, tidal rice cultivation on average had treated the free population of coastal South Carolina and Georgia very well.[17]

Careful readers will note the phrases *wealth per free capita* and *on average*. Throughout the period under study, the entire rice zone of the South Atlantic region featured very sizable slave populations. Slaves constituted 78 percent of the population of the South Carolina low country in 1770, for example, 71 percent of the total population in 1840, and 66 percent of the population as late as 1860. Similarly, in 1860 black slaves constituted about 59 percent of the population in the coastal rice counties of Georgia, the second-most important rice-producing state at the time (together South Carolina and Georgia accounted for 91.6 percent of US production in crop year 1859). Therefore, the phrase *wealth per* free *capita* is employed to account for the many people who were plainly being excluded in these slave-dominated areas.[18]

It is also important to note that the distributions of wealth (and presumably income) were extremely unequal—sometimes astoundingly so—even among the free populations in various parts of the rice region from the early eighteenth century on. Without getting too deep into the intricacies of the statistical measures employed (Gini and Schutz coefficients), both rural and urban areas in the South Atlantic region were among the most unequal in North America. Such conclusions are not altogether surprising given the heavy plantation orientation of the region, as well as the limited availability of suitable swampland, high entry costs, and scale economies in the rice industry. Indeed, operating costs were so high that that of the 4,126 farms of three acres or more in the "rice zone" of South Carolina and Georgia in 1859, only 1608—about 39 percent—grew any rice at all. Rice farming was accordingly concentrated, and, moreover, despite the high average levels of wealth for the free population living in the area, there were a good number of independent landholding farmers and mechanics of modest means in the low country, as well as poor whites both in the "piney woods" and in the region's cities and towns, with limited direct investment in the rice regime. And, of course, a majority of the region's population—capitalized laborers, so to speak—was enslaved and, in material terms, on the margins of subsistence.[19]

Regarding the other side of the coin, rice planters in the South Carolina and Georgia low country were massively overrepresented in the most elite cohort of wealthy Southern slaveholders, with one South Carolina rice planter, Nathaniel Heyward, holding somewhere between 1,829 and 2,340 slaves at the time of his death in 1851, the largest total for any individual in the entire history of the American South. Heyward's total estate in 1851, slaves included, was valued at just over $2 million, equal to $63.9 million in purchasing power today, or, as a proportion of US gross domestic product in 1851, equivalent to $12.8 billion in 2014.[20]

Although no one in the low country was as rich as Heyward, numerous others possessed impressive levels of wealth. Indeed, as William K. Scarborough demonstrates in *Masters of the Big House*, the rice region, its small size and population notwithstanding, was home to an outsized proportion of the South's largest slaveholders. In 1850 twenty-six slaveholders in the United States had slaveholdings of five hundred or more; nine were rice planters in South Carolina and Georgia, with several wealthy sugar cane planters from Louisiana and cotton nabobs from the Mississippi River valley joining Heywood on the antebellum South's master list. Ten years later the number of slaveholders owning five hundred or more slaves had grown to fifty, and fourteen were rice planters along the South Atlantic coast. Not for nothing, then, are the cohesive and confident grandees of the rice country often considered the closest thing to a rural aristocracy that the United

States has ever had. The fact that this elite, by the mid-nineteenth century, had taken on something of a quasihereditary cast at once affirms and punctuates this point.[21]

One can amass evidence almost ad infinitum that the rice economy along the South Atlantic coast generated funds sufficient to enable the free population of this region to achieve very high levels of wealth *on average* between the second half of the eighteenth century and the Civil War.[22] As mentioned above, the words *on average* can conceal as well as reveal, and this is particularly true when it comes to rice production. According to Dale E. Swan's careful sample for crop year 1859, the largest 18 percent of rice growers in coastal South Carolina and Georgia accounted for more than 90 percent of the total rice crop produced, with the top 10 percent producing 72 percent, and with the top 4 percent alone, each accounting for at least a million pounds of rice, accounting for 39 percent. What about smaller producers? The numbers show that the 82 percent of rice growers outside of the elite accounted for just over 9 percent of production in 1859, with two-thirds of all rice growers—the smallest growers—combining to produce just 1 percent of total output.[23]

And slaveholding? Swan finds that for well over a quarter of rice growers—the smallest 28.5 percent measured by capitalization—the modal number of slaves held was but one. By contrast, the largest 36 percent of rice producers, again, measured by capitalization, held at least fifty slaves, with the largest 22 percent averaging at least one hundred. Remember that, in the South as a whole at this time, only 25 percent of free households owned even one slave, with a paltry 3 percent holding twenty or more—the baseline number for planter status.[24]

Despite the importance of "unpacking" averages, the wealth story above is still incomplete, for it is largely a reflection of *stocks* of capital accumulated over extended periods of time rather than about *flows*—revenues, profits, and the like. It is only when such matters are also given their due that one can begin truly to understand the trajectory of the South Atlantic rice region, particularly the roots of its transit from putative staple Eden to commodity hell.

Demand and Supply

The history of the South Atlantic rice region is related closely to, in-deed, in many ways was a function of, global and domestic demand. Rice, however, compared to various small grains and maize, was rela-tively insignificant in most parts of the Western world. To be sure, it has been known in the West since antiquity: rice is mentioned in the Talmud, for example, though not in the Bible (for purposes of com-parison, wheat is mentioned forty-six times in the latter text). Both the Greeks and Romans, moreover, imported rice from India, Persia, and Syria before it was ever grown in the westernmost part of the Eur-asian landmass—that is, Europe—itself. Rice cultivation in Europe first took firm hold in Spain in the eighth century CE and a bit later in southeastern Europe and the Balkans. Andrew Watson referred to these developments as the Arab Agricultural Revolution whereby Arab and other Muslim traders and merchants introduced or at least suc-cessfully diffused crops and crop technology (including rice and rice technology) well beyond the Islamic world.

A number of scholars have recently challenged Watson's general thesis as overstated and in some cases factually wrong. With regard to rice, for example, Michael Decker has pointed out that the cereal traded all over the Roman Empire was "established" as a crop in Roman Egypt in the second century CE, "apparently well established throughout the Mediterranean world" in the fourth century, and even survived the fall of the empire, trading in post-Roman Gaul (France) in the fifth century. The details of the early history of rice in Europe are better left to specialists, though by the medieval period scholars are in agree-ment that the Continent's small rice industry was centered mostly in the Valencia region of Spain. For our purposes, it is perhaps enough to say that rice was traded and grown in Europe for a long time before it first became of more than local importance in economic terms. This happened, experts again agree, in the fifteenth century CE in the north-west of what later became known as Italy. Shortly after rice was estab-lished there, the rich alluvial valleys of Piedmont and Lombardy took off as centers of rice production, and northwest Italy has remained the most important rice-producing region of Europe ever since, followed at a distance by Spain, then, at greater remove, by other producing areas in Portugal, Greece, and France.[25]

At the time of the emergence of the rice industry in Italy, European demand for rice was not great, but it grew gradually in the sixteenth and seventeenth centuries. Demand, such as it was, was met via imports from the Levant (part of the modern Middle East)—small amounts of rice had flowed into Europe from the "East" throughout the medieval period—and, increasingly, from surpluses in Piedmont and Lombardy. One symptom of the economic dynamism of parts of Europe in the early modern period was external commercial expansion, which over time transformed relatively backwater regions into the fulcrum of the modern world. London investors poured capital into the Virginia Company to raise tobacco, and they began to tap—and, in some cases, establish—new, extra-European sources of supply for rice. The first such source was located along the South Atlantic coast of North America. It was, alas, not the last extra-European supplier.

The subject of the European demand for rice, however, is neither straightforward nor necessarily clear, even today. Despite such difficulties, one cannot narrate, let alone interpret the story of rice in the West without some understanding of European demand. In *early* early modern Europe (c. 1500–1650 CE) small quantities of rice were marketed for human food as a supplement to more familiar small grains or as a substitute during shortages. During that same period rice demand was complicated by the fact that the grain also had certain pharmaceutical and ceremonial uses, and among some populations it was apparently considered a luxury or superior good, the demand for which rose disproportionately with income. In Asia, by contrast, rice was often too expensive for the poorest groups, who generally subsisted largely on other cheaper grains and tubers until their incomes reached certain levels, at which time they shifted over rather emphatically to rice.[26]

As time passed, however—certainly by the eighteenth century—the relative importance of rice for ceremonial and pharmaceutical uses or as a luxury product waned, and the cereal was valued more and more as a cheap, versatile grain with a wide variety of alimentary and industrial uses. Rice and rice by-products (broken kernels, husks, bran, etc.) found uses in the starch and paper industries and, importantly, as an animal feed, particularly for swine in in the states that later comprised Germany. The cereal, a mainstay in Asian alcoholic beverages for millennia, gradually found similar uses in Europe. In the eighteenth century, some distilled alcoholic beverages produced in Europe— liqueurs such as brandy in particular—included rice among their ingredients, and Europeans imported small quantities of arrack, often made from fermented rice, from South and Southeast Asia. Later on, of course—by the second half of the nineteenth century—rice and its by-products became important secondary starches for beer brewing in both Europe and America.[27]

Beginning in the eighteenth century, rice found acceptance more and more as an alternative dietary staple (a cheap source of complex carbohydrates) especially important for feeding low-income populations: sailors, prisoners, orphans, soldiers, invalids, the proletariat, and the poor. In this regard it is important to note two further complications. First, part of the demand for rice among the "poor" actually arose because of a rising interest in philanthropic work—what Thomas Haskell refers to as the rising "humanitarian sensibility"—among better-positioned social groups and the state. In a sense, then, the growth in altruism and benevolence, which led eighteenth- and nineteenth-century social reformers and policy makers to purchase cheap, imported food for the poor, helped drive demand for rice as well as other income-elastic "products": namely philanthropy and charity. This phenomenon can be likened to situations today when countries "buy environment"—that is to say, invest heavily in environmental cleanup or protection—as they grow richer.[28]

In addition, it is possible, although unlikely, that rice may have behaved at times in eighteenth- and nineteenth-century Europe and America like what economists refer to as a Giffen good, that is, a good for which demand, counterintuitively, rises with increases in price. Alfred Marshall, for example, focuses on low-quality staples as the quintessential example of Giffen goods, pointing out that "a rise in the price of bread makes so large a drain on the resources of the poorer labouring families and raises so much the marginal utility of money to them, that they are forced to curtail their consumption of meat and the more expensive farinaceous foods: and bread being still the cheapest food which they can get and will take, they consume more, not less of it." To be sure, empirical evidence in the West for the historical existence of a true Giffen good has proven elusive—people are generally able to find a close substitute for the good in question rather than to consume it in greater quantities as its price rises. But evidence has been recently found that rice at times behaved as a Giffen good for the poor in China (Hunan Province).[29] This possibility notwithstanding, such market behavior can also be explained in a perhaps more straightforward way by focusing on future price expectations. That is to say, if consumers believe that prices might spike down the line, they might buy more in the present day even as prices are trending upward.

Markets and market processes, then, are not cut and dried. Accordingly, the Western rice market was quite complex, and the leaders and principals involved in the rice industry in the South Atlantic region seemed over time to misread their place in national and international markets. In introducing students to demand, every economics text discusses the determinants of demand, the most important of which is price, other things being equal. Economists use the Latin term *ceteris paribus* to describe the effect of one economic variable on another, all other things being equal: for example, if demand for a given product outweighs supply, ceteris paribus, prices will rise. Textbook writers quickly point out that if and when other determinants change, the relationship between price and the quantity demanded also changes, resulting in what they call a change in demand. Changes in demand occur when consumers will purchase greater or lesser amounts of a product at a given price, and a small number of determinants are largely responsible for such changes: the number of consumers in the market; consumers' incomes; the prices of related products; consumers' tastes or preferences; and, as suggested above, consumers' future expectations. Changes in any of these determinants can cause a shift in demand for a particular product.

In the case of demand for rice in Europe (and the West generally), a shift—to the right in the demand curve, as economists say—clearly occurred beginning in the eighteenth century. Certainly, population growth, urbanization, and rising incomes in parts of Europe (and the Americas) helped to enlarge the market for rice, and one can find evidence that growing familiarity with the cereal did as well. At particular times and places, price movements increased on related products—small grains, notably—and one can make a case that consumers' future expectations sometimes had similar effects on the rice market.[30]

Markets, of course, are not made by demand alone but by the confluence of demand and supply. What makes the Western rice market particularly interesting is that huge changes appear in rice supply, as with demand, beginning in the eighteenth century. Economists assume, ceteris paribus, that price is the most important consideration influencing the quantity of a good or product supplied (other things being equal). As was the case with demand, other things are not always equal, and certain types of changes can shift the entire supply curve to the left or to the right, meaning that suppliers will supply, in the first case, less and, in the second case, more of a product at any given price. Factors affecting suppliers' costs—other than changes in output of a given product—are generally seen as central to shifts in supply. Among the most important determinants of supply *shifts* are changes in the number of sellers in a given market, changes in technology, input prices, prices of other goods, government policies (taxes, subsidies, etc.), and expectations about future prices.

Regarding rice, technological changes in transportation and communications—both in the eighteenth and especially in the nineteenth century—vastly increased the number of suppliers in the market. Many of the suppliers newly incorporated into the Western rice market operated in areas where input costs and overall cost structures differed significantly from established suppliers, which in turn impacted the geography of supply in profound ways. Changing governmental policies also led to shifts in rice supply, and, certainly, prices of alternative goods and products, as well as future price expectations, helped to explain supply shifts as well. In sum, the Western rice market was marked by dramatic changes on both the demand and supply sides, and the South Atlantic rice region was made and later unmade by these economic factors.[31]

As suggested above, the establishment and early development of the South Atlantic rice industry was an expression par excellence (better than others, in fact) of the economic expansion of early modern Europe. Why par excellence? For starters, the rising demand for foodstuffs in eighteenth-century Europe due to growth in population and income as well as urbanization primed markets. Second, the existence of fertile land or "ghost acres," that is, productive land far from the colonial metropole suitable for export rice production in coastal South Carolina and Georgia. And, third, the equally opportune availability of a seasoned, reasonably priced agricultural labor force— some already experienced in risiculture—the freedom of which was narrowly circumscribed by slavery. A number of scholars have demonstrated that transatlantic shipping also became increasingly efficient in the eighteenth century, communications links improved, and commercial institutions became more sophisticated. Moreover, the fact that the mean size of agricultural units in the rice zone grew significantly over the course of the eighteenth century—in St. Johns Berkeley Parish, South Carolina, one of the leading producing areas at the time, the proportion of slaves living on units with at least thirty slaves increased from 29 percent in the 1720s to 64 percent in the 1770s— suggests that more and more rice was being produced on units subject to economies of scale (which began on estates with thirty or more slaves). All of these considerations helped to promote the rise to prominence—the will to power, as it were—of the rice-exporting economy of the South Atlantic region.[32]

The establishment and development of this staple-producing export platform, virtually all scholars agree today, was also a manifestation of Europe's expanding capitalist economy of the early modern period. If some historians of capitalism continue to engage in rather esoteric debates regarding nomenclature and periodization, few any longer view the plantation colonies established under British auspices in the Americas as anything but capitalist in economic nature and orientation. And fewer still deny that that one of the distinguishing characteristics of capitalism is its dynamism and its capacity for relentless change, even in the swamplands of coastal Carolina.

Roads to Perdition

The solid position that the South Atlantic rice region appeared to have in the second half of the eighteenth century in the most important of these markets—those of northern Europe—began to melt away relatively quickly. The same forces that were responsible for the rise of the rice industry in this region—forces attending the expansion of capitalism and increased market integration—ironically or, perhaps more properly, dialectically were largely responsible for the area's eclipse as a rice-export platform in the first half of the nineteenth century and for its later lapse into stagnation and long-term decline. As was the case with US sugar cane producers a century later, most of the principals in the rice industry—the agricultural capitalists in South Carolina and Georgia and their mercantile and financial confrères in America and abroad—either did not know what hit them, misread market signals and signs, or because of sunk costs and certain inertial features long associated with rice, were very late to respond.[33]

The rice lords' sluggish response was unsurprising. Although economic actors generally respond relatively rationally to market stimuli, we know more and more that "friction" of various sorts often impedes commercial transactions and that market information is often imperfect or at least incomplete, and the costs of accessing the same exceedingly high. Then, too, one must consider the distinction Bernard Bailyn made in 1982 between "manifest" and "latent" historical events, with the former being readily observable to contemporaries and the latter "events that contemporaries were not fully or clearly aware of, at times were not aware of at all, events that they did not consciously struggle over, however much they might have been forced unwittingly to grapple with their consequences, and events that were not recorded as events in the documentation of the time."[34] For example, just as scholars now know with some certainty that increased income and wealth inequality, changing relative prices of foodstuffs, and even climate change likely played roles in various social shocks and upheavals in the early modern period, data readily available today, but less so to contemporaries, allow us better to explain the evolving economic and geographic patterns in the rice industry and trade in the West in the eighteenth and nineteenth centuries.

With the above considerations in mind, it is possible to identify the competitive advantages that explain why the South Atlantic rice region had become by the middle of the eighteenth century the leading supplier of rice on Western markets: a physical environment highly suitable to paddy-rice production; an ample supply of cost-efficient, disciplined, and skilled laborers; and groups of entrepreneurial planters, shippers, and merchants that were able to organize the rice industry with method and rigor. Such advantages, however important, were necessary but insufficient conditions for the long-term health of the region's rice industry. To be sure, South Carolina's magnates enjoyed favorable transportation and communications costs and were comparatively integrated—in what was still an incompletely integrated market for rice—but their dominion would be short lived as new global competitors in the not-too-distant future would outcompete South Carolina and Georgia in the leading markets in the West and, indeed, the world over.[35]

If rice planters in the South Atlantic region in the late eighteenth century believed, averred, and behaved as though the swamps they lorded over were solidly positioned to dominate Western rice markets into the distant future, they were sadly mistaken. In fact, already in the first half of the nineteenth century, the region, despite producing more rice than it ever had before, was overtaken as a supply source in the major markets in the West. Its supersession came about for several reasons, including, for example, internal supply constraints in the area. The tidal rice zone, as discussed earlier, was subject to severe geographical limitations, and, despite the fact that land in paddy maintains soil fertility longer than is the case with many staple crops, fertility did indeed decline markedly on some of the older paddy land in the South Atlantic rice region by the second quarter of the nineteenth century. Then there were problems posed to rice by the rapid expansion in the first half of the nineteenth century of the short-staple cotton industry of the US South. The dynamic growth of this industry not only forced coastal rice planters to compete for outside capital with go-go expansionist cotton planters but also led to a hemorrhaging of capital as well as entrepreneurial talent from the rice zone itself. The opportunity costs of growing paddy rice rose dramatically, as it were, once short-staple cotton made a splash in the South.[36]

There were, then, internal supply constraints. But the main reasons for the relative decline of the South Atlantic rice region had less to do with goings on in the United States than with developments afar. Indeed, the region's rice industry suffered from an arresting convergence of what might be called "causal registers" in the late eighteenth and early nineteenth century—the intensification of maritime trade links between Europe and Asia led to the beginnings of what would soon become a sustained and systematic flow of rice from Asia to Europe. According to Scottish political economist David MacPherson, writing in 1795, rice was in fact the first "necessary" exported to the West from India; all previous exports from India to the West, according to MacPherson, consisted of goods and products that were "rather of ornament and luxury than of use." Rice, by contrast, was very much "necessary" and nothing if not "useful" to a variety of groups and for a variety of reasons in the West.[37]

If India—or, to be more specific, Bengal—accounted for the first large shipments of Asian rice to Europe, exports from South Asia were joined and ultimately far surpassed by shipments from what would later be called Southeast Asia. Such shipments—from Java beginning in the 1820s, from Arakan and Tenasserim beginning in the 1840s and the Irrawaddy-Sittang Delta of Lower Burma beginning in the 1850s, and from Siam and Cochinchina beginning in the 1860s— inundated Western rice markets, swamping and ultimately drowning out completely rice shipments from the South Atlantic rice region of the United States. Rice planters in the low country were not alone in watching foreign imports outstrip US production; Asian indigo, cotton, and sugar made considerable inroads into (and in the case of indigo came to dominate) Western markets in the nineteenth century as well.[38]

The best available evidence suggests that Asian rice rivaled US rice in the leading European markets as early as the 1820s, surpassed US rice in these markets the 1830s, and dominated the same by the 1850s. Total US rice exports were lower by volume in the 1850s than they had been in the 1790s, with the volume and proportion of rice exports destined for European markets falling at faster rates than was the case for the rice exports overall. As time passed, US rice exports were limited more and more to the West Indies and Central and South America, particularly to the late-developing Spanish sugar colonies of Cuba and Puerto Rico. After the Civil War, things got even worse. The United States, despite increasingly high tariffs on Asian rice, was rendered a very large net *importer* of rice right down to World War I.[39] To be sure, the size of the domestic market was growing during the nineteenth century but not sufficiently rapidly to make up for lost export markets and increasing foreign penetration of the domestic market itself. The worm, better yet, the *rice* worm thus turned—and how!

Briefly put, the prevailing—well-nigh universal—view until the late 1980s of how and why the South Atlantic rice industry declined and ultimately collapsed was that its problems came late and quickly and were entirely domestic in nature. But for an article by economist Arthur Cole in 1927, every other authority on the subject attributes the collapse of the industry mainly to the destruction of rice works during the Civil War and labor problems related to emancipation. Those who took the longer view merely added that weather-related problems in the late nineteenth century and early twentieth century (the famous Charleston earthquake of 1886 and several bad hurricanes) provided the death blow, a coup de grâce to an industry whose problems began with the Civil War.[40]

The account offered in this chapter obviously differs strikingly. By broadening the temporal and spatial frame of the story—and, in so doing, rejecting the ruling post hoc, ergo propter hoc (after it, therefore because of it) explanation—things look very different. Since the mid-1980s, this author has been reframing the story, and it is fair to say that today more and more scholars have come to understand that the standard account is at best woefully incomplete. Thus put, the narrative of America's South Atlantic rice industry is one rather more of long-term declension than of precipitous fall.[41]

Evidence other than the absolute and relative decline of rice exports from the South Atlantic region also supports the declension narrative. Despite output growth in the industry in the 1850s, yields were declining, and net rates of return on South Carolina and Georgia rice plantations and farms were largely negative from the 1840s on. The best estimates for the decade of the 1850s as a whole put the return at between negative 4.73 and negative 3.52 percent, with the most careful econometric estimate for crop year 1859 putting the return at an astounding negative 28.3 percent. In retrospect it seems that it was mainly the huge sunk costs in the rice sector—land acquired earlier at great expense, huge investments in irrigation infrastructure and in capitalized labor—and, arguably, the possibility of using rice plantations and farms as platforms for "raising" and selling another commodity, slaves, that kept the South Atlantic rice region in the game for decades.[42]

To be sure, the region's woes were related fundamentally to the fact that global market integration had made it possible for alternative supply sources in Asia to undercut American rice. A number of technological and organizational improvements in transoceanic shipping reduced transport and communications costs significantly and in some cases dramatically over the course of the nineteenth century. Although the advent of steam shipping, the opening of the Suez Canal, and the laying of transoceanic submarine cable are the most celebrated of such improvements, other innovations—improvements in vessel design and loading and unloading technologies, the spread of specialized commercial publications, the advent of steel-hull shipping, and the development of compound and triple-expansion steam engines, and so on—helped cut transport and communications costs, enhance the flow of market information, and reduce friction in transacting trade over long distances. Britain's domination of the global seas and trade networks helped reduce insurance costs while reductions in gun/ton and men/ton ratios helped bring down shipping costs as well.[43]

None of these developments themselves would have necessarily harmed the South Atlantic rice region—indeed, in principle, they could have helped the industry to expand. But in a real historical sense they certainly did, by creating the possibility for formidable new competitors to enter, penetrate, and ultimately dominate the leading Western rice markets. Scholars are still debating precisely why and how South Asian and Southeast Asian rice producers—the vast majority of whom were peasant proprietors or tenants—were able to outcompete large-scale agricultural capitalists in the West. Various interpretations abound even today. Marx long ago pointed to the fact that "windfalls" of major significance (land, resources, energy, etc.) often resulted from the effective linkage of precapitalist or noncapitalist economies to the West, because land and labor costs were but a fraction of such costs in the West. Numerous scholars on the left, building on Marx's insights, continue to work within or at least with this interpretive framework. In this regard, proponents of "articulation of production modes" approaches and advocates of the "anticommodity" line have made significant interventions as well, arguing that export crops in less developed economies often owe their cost advantages to the fact that producers are only partially in the world economy. More specifically, they contend that the low prices (or wages) producers of export crops receive arise from power asymmetries and from the fact such producers are in effect being cross-subsidized by subsistence producers (often in the same family).

Non-Marxist, indeed, anti-Marxists such as the Burmese development economist Hla Myint have placed a somewhat more benign spin on the low cost structure of the Southeast Asian rice industry, pushing what is now known as a "vent-for-surplus" line, which is to say that new market opportunities to export rice drew unused or underutilized land and labor into production, which in turn benefited producers economically to some degree, however paltry levels of remuneration may appear from some vantage points. And, of course, the fact that many rice producers in fertile, well-watered Bengal and South-

east Asia were already experienced and relatively efficient agriculturalists did not hurt their positions either. At the end of the day, these
Asian producers and the supply chains that developed to enlist—if
not necessarily to accommodate—them were able to provide rice for
sale in Europe and in North America (as early as the late 1830s) at
prices significantly lower than that of domestically grown US rice.[44]

Earlier this chapter invoked what Bernard Bailyn has referred to as
"latent" historical events and phenomena to help to make the argument regarding the evolution of the Western rice market and South
Carolina and Georgia's place within it. Truth be told, the phenomena
discussed above were not completely latent. Knowledgeable rice traders and merchants, the commercial press, and even a few keen-eyed
and hard-nosed rice planters in the South Atlantic states knew which
way the wind was blowing. You do not have to be a weatherman, after
all, to spot the storm clouds on the horizon. As early as the 1820s,
there are scattered references to the fact that "East Indian" rice was
selling almost everywhere in the West at considerably lower prices
than US rice, generally 20–25 percent lower or even more. The problem was not one of observation but of interpretation. Until the late
nineteenth century, rice leaders and industry principals in Carolina
and Georgia continued to cling to the belief that consumers in the
market would pay a premium for "Carolina" rice, particularly the
Carolina Gold variety, because of its superior quality as compared with
all other varieties of rice throughout the world. Unfortunately, they
failed to grasp the fact that perceived quality—tastes and preferences
are subjective, after all—was not all that important a consideration
given the purposes to which rice was put. Few working-class consumers of rice in the West—and few of their charity benefactors—would
pay a price premium for quality. Quality mattered even less, moreover, when rice was used for industrial purposes or to feed cattle or
slop pigs. Most rice planters in the United States were not worried,
however, until it was too late. Hindsight is of course 20-20, yet David
Doar, one of the last great rice planters in South Carolina, writing in
the 1920s—long after the South Atlantic rice industry had faded away,
that is to say—finally got it. "Our rice," he wrote, "was finer, the best in

the world, but when it came to buying, the rice-eater would take cheapness instead of quality every time." This insight, however accurate, might have made a difference had it come eighty or even ninety years before.[45]

Commodity Hell

By the late antebellum period, the U.S. rice industry had begun its fall into commodity hell. It moved deeper and deeper into this inferno after the Civil War, and, like Dante's—albeit allegorical—descent, the economy of the region plunged toward perdition. Although there were numerous reasons for the economic collapse of the region in the late nineteenth century—wartime destruction and the summary loss without compensation of a huge proportion of white personal wealth through slave emancipation—one of the principal reasons for the collapse of the low country lay in its dogged commitment to risiculture. From its colonial beginnings, the entire region was built by and for rice and pretty much rice alone. By the mid- to late nineteenth century, this fertile but environmentally challenging—and limited—region offered the population, white and black alike, few viable economic alternatives. Phosphates and fertilizer in some areas, lumbering, maybe a little truck farming, later, tourism, but not much else for a long, long time. Thus, a region that was once so rich had by 1900 become the poorest part of the poorest census region in the United States, there to remain for decades. Only with the coming of World War II did the structure of opportunity in the area begin to change for the better, generations after the demise of rice. Commodity hell, thus, proved protracted though not eternal for the inhabitants of the South Atlantic coast after their economic mainstay was gone.[46]

Writers on commoditization today often offer up lists of "early warning signs" that a product is entering into dangerous, even hellish market terrain. For example, in *Commoditization and the Strategic Response*, business consultant Andrew Holmes sees seven such signs:

1. Increasing competition
2. Prevalence of me-too products and services

3. A belief that all suppliers are fundamentally the same
4. The decreasing desire on the customer's part to look at new or differentiating options or features
5. An increasing preference for customers to select on the basis of price and little else
6. A reluctance for customers to pay for anything they consider unnecessary
7. Increasing pressures on margins[47]

Alas, all of these signs were present in the South Atlantic rice industry in the mid-nineteenth century, hiding in plain sight.

For all their colonial wealth and magnificent mansions, however, the leaders and principals involved in the South Atlantic rice industry were unable to escape commodity hell, and the industry died a slow, lingering death, finally expiring in the early twentieth century. American agricultural capitalism and agricultural capitalists did not die with it, however, and, as the life was going out of the industry in the Southeast, a completely new rice industry, based on different principles—the most important of which were scale, capital intensity, and minimal labor inputs—was rising in the Old Southwest, that is, in southwestern Louisiana, southeastern Texas, and east central Arkansas, and a bit later in the Sacramento Valley of California. In the Old Southwest, ironically, the new rice industry was built not by Southerners but by agricultural entrepreneurs, most of whom had migrated south from the Midwest. The new rice industry, established on a different, sounder footing, as it were, could and eventually did compete effectively against Asian rice on Western, indeed, world markets, albeit with a little help from its (governmental) friends. But that is a story for another time, another place.[48]

SVEN BECKERT

Cotton and the US South

❧

A Short History

THE HISTORY OF THE US SOUTH in the nineteenth century is the history of cotton.[1] Cotton growing was the most significant economic activity of Southerners, the American South mattered to the national and global economy because of its cotton, and the greatest political crisis of the United States in the nineteenth century, the Civil War, concerned the social, political, and economic structure that enabled the South's culture of cotton. At the heart of that conflict was the question of whether a cotton-growing regime sustained by slave labor should be able to expand territorially and whether the South's particular form of slave-based capitalism should enjoy the protections of the federal government. When South Carolina Senator and cotton planter James Henry Hammond argued famously on the floor of the Senate in 1858 that "cotton *is* king," he comprehended one of the central dynamics of the Southern and global economy.

So central has cotton become to the image of the American South that many Americans tend to forget that the Southern states came to cotton quite late—toward the end of the eighteenth century—and also quite suddenly, with the invention of the cotton gin in 1793. Cotton's global history is long and complicated, but it was only in the 1790s that aspiring American planters combined European capital, expropriated lands, and enslaved workers of African heritage to begin growing cotton for world markets. It was a move that did more than reshape the Southern countryside from forests, meadows, and swamps into vast cotton farms; it also had a tremendous impact on the larger world, spurring rapid industrialization in western Europe and New England. It enriched merchants throughout the Atlantic world, and the wealth of cities such as New York and Liverpool, Le Havre and Mulhouse, Bremen and Lowell was to a significant degree produced in Southern cotton fields. Merchants in these cities accumulated riches in the global cotton trade, and this capital, in turn, eventually fueled the emergence of other industries and banks. It even transformed the economies of India and the Ottoman Empire, as their position in the global cotton economy shifted in reaction to the rise of a US-fueled European cotton-manufacturing industry. As the supplier of the raw materials for the most dynamic metropolitan industry of the century, the American South was indeed the backbone of the first great phase of capitalist industrialization that began to spread across Europe and the northern United States. It was one of the core connections that explain the North Atlantic's "great divergence," the moment in the late eighteenth and early nineteenth centuries when it became much wealthier than other parts of the world.

"Hashish of the West"

From almost any angle, cotton was important to the mid-nineteenth-century South and vice versa. Unlike rice, tobacco, or sugar cane, which were important though regionally focused industries, cotton stretched from the Atlantic coast to the Mississippi River and beyond. Hundreds of thousands of African American laborers worked the Cotton Kingdom. Indeed, the vast majority of nineteenth-century Southern slaves ultimately labored on cotton plantations. The most significant export of the United States as a whole was Southern-grown cotton, indeed so much so that by 1860, 60 percent of all US exports consisted of cotton. The American South was also, by far, the most important source for the Western world's most crucial raw material. By the late 1850s, the Southern states accounted for nearly 100 percent of the 374 million pounds of cotton used in the United States, a full 77 percent of the 800 million pounds processed in Britain, 90 percent of the 192 million pounds used in France, 60 percent of the 115 million pounds spun in German Zollverein, and as much as 92 percent of the 102 million pounds manufactured in Russia.[2] Cotton had become so central to the prosperity of the Atlantic world that poet John Greenleaf Whittier called it the "Hashish of the West." It was like a drug that created powerful hallucinatory dreams of territorial expansion, of judges who decide that "right is wrong," and of heaven as "a snug plantation" with "angels" as "negro overseers."[3] The importance of Southern cotton to the global economy in the nineteenth century can be compared only to the world's dependence on Middle Eastern oil a century later.

Cotton became important to the American South because this "white gold" had become central to the global economy. Before 1800, producing cotton cloth was mostly a local pursuit. Millions of farmers cultivated small amounts of cotton, which they then spun by hand and finally wove into fabric on simple looms. After 1780, however, with the onset of the Industrial Revolution, production became mechanized, and the geographic distances between cotton growers, spinners, weavers, and consumers increased drastically. For the next hundred years, cotton was so important to the global economy that no other manufacturing industry employed as many people. By inventing the factory as the most efficient way of producing textiles, cotton manufacturers also recast the way humans worked. By searching for ever more hands to staff their factories, English, American, Brazilian, and Japanese cotton manufacturers, among others, encouraged unprecedented movement from the countryside into cities. Likewise, by demanding ever more cotton to feed their hungry factories in Lancashire and elsewhere, manufacturers and merchants stimulated planters to vastly expand cotton lands. And the need for cheap labor to work all that land led to the forced migration of hundreds of thousands of slaves, as well as the colonization of new territories in Asia and Africa. By producing ever more cotton textiles ever more efficiently and selling them to markets throughout the world, these American and European cotton traders inadvertently destroyed less efficient indigenous ways of producing textiles and in the process decisively moved the center of the cotton textile industry from Asia to western Europe and the United States. In their search for labor, capital, land, raw materials, and consumers, these nineteenth-century capitalists brought together different world regions—creating, in fact, one of the earliest globally integrated industries.

During the nineteenth century, cotton was important in numerous places. In Britain, it became a significant manufacturing industry, with raw cotton its biggest import and cloth and yarn a crucial export. In India, shifts within its huge cotton industry—away from spinning and weaving and toward the growing of cotton for export—combined with the loss of its export markets for finished cotton goods created tectonic upheavals in the region's economy. In Continental Europe, cotton became the first mechanized large-scale manufacturing industry. In the United States, raw cotton exports established the young nation's place in the global economy. In Mexico, Egypt, India, and Brazil, the first tentative steps toward domestic industrialization were taken with cotton. Egyptian agriculture was turned into a huge and increasingly monocultural cotton-growing system, focusing on export production. By the late nineteenth and early twentieth centuries, peasants throughout Africa, northern Argentina, Australia, and elsewhere—under pressure from metropolitan governments and capitalists—converted their fields into cotton plantations. Huge profits, meanwhile, were amassed by many merchant and banking families whose names are still familiar today: Baring, Rothschild, Ward, Brown, Rathbone, Volkart, Reinhardt, Knoop, Birla, Tata. Throughout the world, consumer demand for cotton textiles grew too, and especially in areas that came late to cotton, such as Europe, this cotton-manufacturing boom revolutionized how people dressed and how they kept clean. This truly was the era when cotton was king.

Global Networks

The history of cotton in the American South depended on cotton's role in the wider world. For about nine hundred years—between 1000 CE and 1900 CE—cotton was the world's most important manufacturing industry. Originating in South Asia, eastern Africa, and Central America at least five millennia ago, the crop and its manufacture into fabric had spread into most regions of the world by the year 1000 CE. Vibrant artisanal cotton manufacturing complexes emerged, and although they mostly focused on satisfying the need among the growers and producers themselves for yarn and cloth, they also served distant markets. For instance, Indian cottons traveled to Southeast Asia, East Africa, and the Middle East and even showed up in Europe as early as the Roman Empire. Kano, in present day Nigeria, supplied the needs of the people of the Sahara. Aztec cotton goods found their way into what is today the territory of the United States. In the sixteenth century, Europeans, who until this time mostly depended on woolens and linens, began to develop a taste for exotic cotton fabrics and came increasingly to dominate this intercontinental trade. They would export South Asian cotton fabric both to sell to European consumers and to exchange for slaves in Africa. It was at this time, also, that Europeans began to produce cotton textiles themselves, though their share of the global output remained miniscule.

This ancient industry was to undergo a radical shift in the late eighteenth century, as British mechanics invented a fundamentally new way of spinning yarn and—eventually, a few decades later—of weaving cloth. These machines, among them the spinning jenny, the water frame, and the spinning mule, increased human productivity in unprecedented ways. Cotton manufacturing, for the first time, came to be concentrated in Europe.

Such European dominance was the result not just of the mechanical genius of British artisans but also of successful European insertion into and then domination of global networks. The scope of these networks was astonishing. Raw cotton, for example, arrived in huge quantities from distant places, mostly North America but also the West Indies and South America, enabling Europe to overcome its resource constraints by making use of what Kenneth Pomeranz (and the previous chapter) called "ghost acres," that is, land outside of Europe that could be transformed for the production of agricultural commodities for European markets without leading to upheaval in the European countryside itself. The labor that went into the growing of cotton was mostly that of slaves, forcefully deported from yet another part of the world, Africa. Some technologies that were important to the manufacturing process, especially as they related to the crucial dyeing of fabrics, were laboriously copied from Indian artisans. Global networks also affected markets for the finished product, both within Europe and abroad. Domestically, the market for cotton textiles in Europe had expanded as a result of the greater availability of Indian fabrics in the wake of European expansion to that part of the world. And the enormously elastic markets that encouraged British merchants and manufacturers to invest in the fledging new techniques of cotton manufacturing in the first place were largely to be found abroad, first in Africa, Continental Europe, and the Americas, and later in Asia, India primarily. Right from the beginning, global connections, and the ability of European states and capitalists to reshape them, were essential to the emergence of the European cotton textile industry. And one of these connections, a particularly important one, was with the American South.

But how did the US South come to play such a decisive role in the history of cotton? Its arrival to global cotton production is not a straightforward story. Since very little cotton grew in Europe, its young cotton-manufacturing industry depended entirely on its supply of raw materials from non-European sources. At first, in the early eighteenth century, European traders bought cotton from local merchants in the port cities of the Ottoman Empire, especially Izmir, but once demand exploded that supply proved to be insufficient. At the same time, the ability of European capital to recast the Ottoman countryside to facilitate increased production of cotton for export was limited. They found it extremely difficult to persuade peasants to focus their labor on producing cotton for world markets. In fact, in much of the world, European capitalists and statesmen were unable to dispossess rural cultivators from their land or from control over their labor and were incapable of undermining their long-ingrained subsistence strategies. The social power of peasants successfully restricted (but did not preclude) their involvement with production for long-distance markets; state-sponsored coercion was often required to make the transition to world market production possible.

As a result of this difficulty in gaining access to inexpensive cotton from independent peasant producers in the Ottoman Empire, European capitalists turned westward. They looked to new areas of the world—particularly the Americas—and to new methods of labor mobilization—slavery, above all—to slake their demand. At first, cotton growers in the West Indies and Brazil were able to satisfy the rapidly growing hunger of European cotton mills. Planters there applied the lessons they had learned in the growing of tobacco, rice, and, especially, sugar to cotton. Specifically, they applied extraordinary violence to solve the problem of persuading rural cultivators to grow cotton for world markets at ever lower prices. But this Caribbean and Brazilian cotton-growing nexus also soon reached its limits of production, especially in the 1790s when supply was curtailed by slaves rebelling on the Caribbean's most important cotton island, Saint-Domingue, present-day Haiti. When demand for cotton simultaneously shot up in England and France, prices for cotton skyrocketed.

This convergence of factors propelled the United States into the global cotton market. Before 1790, very little US cotton was produced for trade and very little was exported to Britain, indeed so little, that when in 1785 American-grown cotton arrived in the port of Liverpool, the customs authorities confiscated it, saying that it could not possibly be the product of the United States. In very short order, and especially after Eli Whitney invented a new kind of cotton gin in 1793, which allowed for a more efficient removal of seeds of American upland cotton, US cotton was able to capture world markets, dominating them for the next century and beyond. Like the spinning and water frame, which transformed the manufacture of cotton cloth (and other technological breakthroughs studied elsewhere in this book), Whitney's gin overcame a key bottleneck to production, and his easily imitated invention increased productivity by a factor of fifty. Overnight, the invention of Whitney's gin transformed American cotton, triggering what can only be described as a "cotton rush," with land on which cotton grew reputedly trebling in price. The transformation was stag-

gering: in 1800, 25 percent of the cotton unloaded in Liverpool originated from the United States; twenty years later, that number had increased to 59 percent, and, in 1850, a full 72 percent of cotton consumed
in Britain was grown in the United States.[4]

Continental Consolidation

Why the United States? What was its competitive advantage? When in
the 1790s demand for cotton exploded at the same time West Indian
production diminished, the United States was the one area in the
world in which emptied lands, plentiful bonded labor, and a politically
influential planter class existed. In the areas where cotton was to be
grown, no powerful and entrenched social structure needed to be dis-
lodged. Instead, indigenous inhabitants were forcefully removed and
workers forcefully moved in, leaving planters free to recast nature and
reorganize labor as they wished. It is hard, if not impossible, to image
that such a transformation of land and labor for the cultivation of cotton could have been effected anywhere else in the world. Indeed,
when the British tried to increase cotton production for export in
India in the 1820s and 1830s, they largely failed. Production in other
parts of the world, such as the West Indies, Brazil, and the Ottoman
Empire, also did not expand. The British economist J. T. Danson, in an
1857 article entitled "On the Existing Connection between American
Slavery and the British Cotton Manufacture" in the *Quarterly Journal
of the Statistical Society*, concluded that "there is not, and never has
been, any considerable source of supply for cotton, . . . which is not
obviously and exclusively maintained by slave-labour." Herman
Merivale, British colonial bureaucrat, agreed in 1840, finding that
Manchester's and Liverpool's "opulence is as really owing to the toil
and suffering of the negro, as if his hands had excavated their docks
and fabricated their steam-engines."[5]

Central to the global economy and spectacularly profitable, the
cotton economy of the American South expanded rapidly throughout
the first decades of the nineteenth century. In 1790, three years before Whitney's invention, the United States had produced 1.5 million

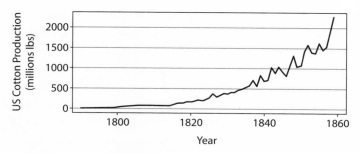

Cotton Production in the United States, 1790–1900 (in million pounds). "Hay, Cotton, Cottonseed, Shorn Wool, and Tobacco—Acreage, Production, and Price: 1790 to 1970—Con.," in *Historical Statistics of the United States, Colonial Times to 1970*, by the US Department of Commerce, part 1 (Washington, DC: Government Printing Office, 1975), 517–518.

pounds of cotton; in 1800 that number grew to 36.5 million pounds, and in 1820 to 167.5 million pounds. By 1802 the United States was already the single-most important supplier of cotton to the British market, and by 1857 the United States would produce about as much cotton as China, the world's leading producer until then.[6]

As more and more land was plowed under to plant cotton, a crop that rapidly exhausted the soil, production spread farther west and farther south, facilitated again by newly emptied lands, portable slave labor, and ginning technology that allowed cotton agriculture to be easily transferred to new territories. Unlike the Egyptian, Sea Island, or Pima cotton that grew in the coastal South Atlantic region—where in places it even rivaled the dominion of rice—upland cotton could be grown in diverse locations. All the plant needed was warmth, rainfall, and fertile soil. The cotton belt, sweeping from central South Carolina to east Texas, provided an almost perfect environment for the upland species, and, once the technological issue of separating lint and seed had been resolved, cotton farming spread like a feverish epidemic across the hot and humid Southern landscape.[7]

Agronomists contributed directly to the cotton revolution, crossing plant varieties to produce robust and adaptable plants that yielded high volumes of more readily picked cotton—enslaved workers in the

1830s, for instance, could pick twice the amount of Mexican cotton than older Green Seed varieties. In addition to the superior yield, picking, and disease resistance, the newer varieties had higher lint-to-seed ratios than the plants they replaced, and their widespread introduction was of vital importance to the expansion of the plantation frontier. This happened particularly at times when cotton prices rose. While the price of cotton gradually declined over the first half of the nineteenth century, sharp price upswings—such as in the first half of the 1810s, between 1832 and 1837, and again after the mid-1840s—produced expansionist bursts. In 1811, one-sixteenth of all cotton grown in the United States came from states and territories west of South Carolina and Georgia; by 1820 that share had reached one-third, and, in 1860, three-fourths. New cotton fields sprouted in the sediment-rich lands along the banks of the Mississippi, the upcountry of Alabama, and the black prairie of Arkansas. So rapid was this move westward that, by the end of the 1830s, Mississippi was producing more cotton than any other Southern state.[8]

Such territorial expansion of cotton agriculture was aided by culture and history. Ever since the first European settlers stepped off their boats, they had been pushing inland. In the late eighteenth century, Native Americans still controlled substantial territories only a few hundred miles inland from the coastal provinces, yet they were unable to stop the white settlers' steady encroachment. The settlers eventually won a bloody and centuries-long war that succeeded in turning the land of Native Americans into land that was legally "empty," a land without most of its people and thus without the entanglements of historically developed social structures. In terms of unencumbered land, the South had no rival in the cotton-growing world.

With the support of Southern politicians, the federal government aggressively secured new territory by acquiring land from foreign powers and from forced cessions of Native Americans. In 1803, the Louisiana Purchase nearly doubled the territory of the United States, in 1819 the United States acquired Florida from Spain, and in 1845 it annexed Texas—all of which contained lands superbly suited to cotton agriculture. While there were many reasons for expansion—cotton being just one—it is difficult to imagine the US rise to world cotton supremacy without these land grabs. Indeed, by 1850, 67 percent of US cotton grew on land that had not been part of the United States half a century earlier.[9]

If the project of continental consolidation provided access to new cotton lands, it also secured major rivers needed to carry the harvested cotton. America's remarkably cheap transportation costs were the direct result of the expansion of its national territory. Most significant was the Mississippi, whose surge of cotton freight turned New Orleans, at the river's mouth, into the key American cotton port. But other rivers—the Red River in Louisiana and the Tombigbee and Mobile in Alabama—mattered as well. The first steamboats appeared on the Mississippi in 1817, cheapening transport costs, and, by the 1830s, railroads connected much of this newly acquired and settled hinterland to rivers and seaports. The Southern style of railroad construction with tracks laid from farm to port, amplified these decisive advantages in transportation infrastructure.[10]

To work these new fields, planters moved thousands of slaves into cotton-producing territories, many from the states of the Upper South, where tobacco agriculture was in a downward spiral. In the 1790s, the slave population of the state of Georgia, for example, nearly doubled, to sixty thousand. In South Carolina, the number of slaves in the upcountry cotton-growing districts grew from twenty-one thousand in 1790 to seventy thousand twenty years later, including fifteen thousand slaves newly deported from Africa.[11] All the way to the Civil War, cotton and slavery would expand in lockstep.

Cotton, until the advent of mechanized harvesting during the 1940s, was a labor-intensive crop. "[T]he true limitation upon the production of cotton," argued the Southern journal *De Bow's Review*, "is labor." And planters in the United States—unlike elsewhere—enjoyed access to large supplies of cheap labor, which the *American Cotton Planter* called in 1853 "the cheapest and most available labor in the world." In the United States, nearly any labor shortage could be fixed with the right amount of money, and the slave markets in New Orleans and elsewhere boomed along with cotton. As significant, hundreds of thousands of slaves already in the United States were available to grow cotton because tobacco production in the states of the Upper South became less profitable after the American Revolution, encouraging slave owners there to sell their human property. As one British observer remarked perceptively in 1811, "[T]he cultivation of tobacco in Virginia and Maryland, has been less of late an object of attention; and the gangs of negroes formerly engaged in it, have been sent into the southern states, where the American cotton planter, thus reinforced, is enabled to commence his operations with increasing vigour." Indeed, by 1830 a full one million people (or one in thirteen Americans) grew cotton in the United States. Most of them were enslaved.[12]

The expansion of cotton production not only led to an enormous shift of slave labor from the Upper to the Lower South, but it also reinvigorated the institution of slavery in North America. In the thirty years after the invention of the cotton gin alone (between 1790 and 1820), a quarter-million slaves were forcefully relocated from other parts of North America; between 1783 and the closing of the international slave trade in 1808, traders imported an estimated 170,000 slaves into the United States, accounting for one-third of all slaves imported into North America since 1619. By 1860, the internal slave trade had moved up to a million slaves forcefully to the Deep South, most to grow cotton.[13]

To be sure, not all cotton in the United States was grown by slaves on large plantations. Free small farmers in the Southern upcountry produced cotton as well, and they did so because it provided ready cash and its cultivation, unlike the growing of sugar or rice, did not require significant capital investments. Yet, despite their efforts, in aggregate they produced only a small share of the total crop. In 1860, for instance, 85 percent of all Southern cotton was grown on farms larger than one hundred acres; the planters who owned those farms owned 91.2 percent of all slaves. The cotton crop was overwhelmingly tended by slaves, and, in areas where large quantities of cotton was grown, there were relatively few white farmers. The larger the farm, the better the planter was able to take advantage of the economies of scale inherent in slave-based cotton production. For instance, only larger farms could afford the gins to remove seeds and presses to compress loose cotton into tightly pressed bales to lower shipping costs. Big operations could also engage in agricultural experiments to wrest more nutrients from cleared soil, and they could buy more slaves to avoid the labor constraints that so limited the expansion of cotton farms elsewhere in the world.[14]

In addition to access to expropriated lands and the violent domination of labor, the nearly complete control of the state by cotton lords also helps explain how the United States gained such a competitive advantage in the emerging global empire of cotton. The Yazoo-Mississippi Delta offers a telling example of how these three factors came together to promote US dominance in the cotton trade, starting with its geography. For millennia, in an area of approximately seven thousand square miles, the mighty Mississippi had offloaded its rich sediments as it flowed to the Gulf of Mexico, creating a seedbed that would become the world's most productive cotton-growing land. In 1859, as many as sixty thousand Delta slaves produced a staggering sixty-six million pounds of cotton, nearly ten times as much as was exported from Saint-Domingue to France during the height of its production in the early 1790s.[15]

For the Delta to become the chief grower of the industrial world's most important commodity—a kind of Saudi Arabia of the early nineteenth century—its land had to be taken from its original inhabitants, and labor, capital, knowledge, and state power had to be mobilized in the service of profit. Between 1820 and 1832, a series of treaties backed by skirmishes and armed confrontations transferred much of the land from the Choctaws—its native inhabitants—to white settlers. Using wagons, rafts, and flatboats, hopeful cotton planters brought slaves from elsewhere in the South to clear that land of its "jungle-like" vegetation and later to hoe the soil, sow seeds, prune the young plants, and then harvest the cotton. The news that the Delta was "the most certain cotton planting area in the world" spread through the South; planters who were able to draw on sufficient capital (mostly in the form of labor since the land itself was cheap) and expertise moved in. The plantations they built became substantial businesses. By 1840,

Washington County, in the heart of the Delta, counted more than ten slaves for every white inhabitant. By 1850, each and every white family in the county owned on average more than 80 slaves. The largest Delta planter, Stephen Duncan, owned 1,036 slaves, and the value of his property by the late 1850s was estimated at $1.3 million (the equivalent of $36.5 million in 2014). While not typical cotton farms, which were often much smaller and worked by fewer slaves, plantations in the Delta were highly capitalized businesses—indeed among the very largest in North America—and the investments necessary to operate such plantations were beyond the reach of many Northern industrialists. Wealth, as viewed from the front porches of the lavish and elegantly furnished mansions in the Delta, appeared to flow out of the soil, the result of a strange alchemy that combined emptied lands, slave labor, a supportive state, and, as discussed below, the never ending flow of European capital.[16]

Cotton, Capital, and Slavery

The growing domination of global cotton markets by US planters, in fact, was self-sustaining. As cotton growth expanded in the Southern United States and as British and eventually Continental European consumers became more and more dependent on that supply, institutional links between the South and Europe—especially Liverpool, Le Havre, and Bremen—deepened. For their part, European merchants based in Charleston, Memphis, and New Orleans built a dense network of shipping connections that integrated the trade in cotton with their other businesses. People engaged in the cotton trade crossed the North Atlantic frequently, forging close business connections, friendships, and even marriages. Such networks, in turn, made transatlantic trade more secure and more predictable and thus lowered costs, giving the United States another decisive advantage over its potential competitors, including India and Brazil.

These networks operated by sending cotton from the United States to Europe and capital in the opposite direction. This capital, more often than not, was secured by mortgages on slaves, giving the owners of these mortgages the right to a particular slave should the debtor default. As historian Bonnie Martin has shown, in Louisiana during the national period, 88 percent of loans secured by mortgages used slaves as (partial) collateral; in South Carolina it was 82 percent. In total, she estimates that hundreds of millions of dollars of capital was secured by human property. Slavery thus not just allowed for the rapid allocation of labor but also for a swift allocation of capital.[17]

With enormous riches gained from expropriated land and labor, planters invested in agricultural improvements, another illustration of how success begot further success. They experimented, for example, with various cotton hybrids, crossing Indian, Ottoman, Central American, and West Indian seeds to create cotton strains adapted to particular local climates and soils. Most significant were the cotton seeds brought from Mexico in 1806 by Natchez planter Walter Burling. This variety produced larger bolls that could be picked by hand more easily and, according to experts, "possessed better fiber quality, especially fiber length, and was resistant to 'rot.'"[18]

Since the expansion of cotton agriculture depended on the advance of credit, often secured by mortgages on slaves and most of which derived from the London money market, plantation patterns began to follow the competitive logic of markets rather than the whimsy of personal aspiration and regional circumstance. The rhythm of industrial production entered the plantation, and capital moved to wherever cotton could be produced in the greatest quantities and at the lowest cost. To the great lament of Southern planters, much of their wealth and power was dependent on merchants—who could sell planters' cotton, supply them with goods, and provide them credit— and on the London money market. But this was not a one-way street: the London money market and the Lancashire manufacturers depended just as much on the planters—as the local experts in the violent expropriation of land and labor—for their wealth and power. The old paternalism of East Coast planters, shielded partially by the mercantilist logic of mutually beneficial and protected exchange between motherland and colony of the greater British imperial economy, had given way to a more competitive and fluid social order mediated by merchant capital.[19]

So important had American cotton become to the Western world that in 1897 a German economist remarked in retrospect that "a disappearance of the American North or West would have been of less significance to the world, than the elimination of the South." Southern planters, convinced of their central role in the global economy, gleefully announced that they held "THE LEVER THAT WIELDS THE DESTINY OF MODERN CIVILIZATION." And their incredible success also served as a self-justification of not merely the necessity but also the rightness of slavery. As cotton became central to ever more manufacturers, a world without slavery became ever less imaginable to cotton industrialists and statesmen. As the *American Cotton Planter* put it in 1853, "[T]he slave-labor of the United States, has hitherto conferred and is still conferring inappreciable blessings on mankind. If these blessings continue, slave-labor must also continue, for it is idle to talk of producing Cotton for the world's supply with free labor. It has never yet been successfully grown by voluntary labor."[20]

This cotton-slavery nexus remained fabulously profitable for many decades. But it also contained within itself tensions that led to its eventual demise. Most important was the fact that slavery was fundamentally unstable. Slavery, after all, relied on violence, and the contest between labor lords and workers could turn at any point, as it did, indeed, in Saint-Domingue in the 1790s. As the cotton industry became increasingly important to European economies, concerns about the stability of its foundation—the institution of slavery—came to the fore. Slavery, manufacturers understood, was at the root of their prosperity, but simultaneously it was a source of constant worry. Saint-Domingue was, after all, in the living memory of many.

Just as potentially disruptive were the emerging political conflicts within the United States itself. The political needs of slave owners, which were directly related to containing the tensions fundamental to the relationship between slaves and masters, increasingly diverged from those of Americans who were profiting from the emerging industrial capitalism in the Northern states of the Union.[21] Eventually, as we all know, this disagreement destabilized the institution of slavery, and with it the world's dominant cotton-producing system came into crisis by the 1860s. The outbreak of Civil War on the North American continent jeopardized future supplies of slave-grown cotton for the factories of Europe. Without slave-grown cotton pouring out of the ports of the US South, Europe's most important industry came to a standstill.

So important was cotton grown in the South that the American Civil War marked, among other things, one of the most important events in the history of global capitalism. The world's first true raw-materials crisis brought to a halt hundreds of factories and hundreds of thousands of workers in the industrial areas of England, France, Germany, Switzerland, and Russia. Workers streamed through the streets of prominent cotton-milling towns such as Oldham, UK, and Mulhouse, France, calling for cotton supplies or relief. The war in North America led to frantic efforts by European governments to secure cotton from different areas of the world. Government bureaucrats and rulers in Paris, Berlin, Moscow, and London poured over maps to figure out who in the world could replace slaves in the American South and might grow cotton for export. And in the South itself the inability to sell the Confederacy's only globally competitive product—cotton—resulted in a severe balance-of-payments crisis, inflation, and a rapid hollowing out of the entire economy of the breakaway region.

Radical Restructuring

One of the most significant results of the war was a radical restructuring of the South's, but also the world's, major industry—cotton. In fact, a key lesson of the Civil War was that labor, more than land, constrained the production of cotton.[22] Emancipation of slaves in the American South, therefore, was recognized as being potentially threatening not only to North American cotton growers but also to the well-being of European industry. With slavery in the world's most important cotton-growing areas abolished, a top question in the offices of European statesmen and capitalists was how to secure cotton without slavery. Emancipation, for them, meant the need to invent a new system of labor to produce cotton. What would that new system be? How could free rural cultivators be organized, mobilized, and motivated to grow the white gold and move it to market, whether in the United States or elsewhere in the world?

At first, pessimism reigned. Antebellum experiences suggested that such a transition would be difficult, since nonslave cotton had arrived only in small quantities in the ports of Liverpool, Bremen, and Le Havre. Cotton manufacturers understood that at prevailing antebellum world market prices, few cultivators in India, Brazil, Africa, or, for that matter, the American South, could produce very much cotton for European markets. Rural cultivators in control of both their labor and land—whether in India, Africa, Egypt, or even the upcountry of the Southern United States—usually had resisted growing cotton for world markets at prices competitive with slave-grown cotton. Moreover, and in singular contrast to emancipation on US sugar cane estates, efforts by cotton planters to rely on wage workers failed, as cultivators the world over refused to work for wages on cotton plantations. As Timothy Mitchell puts it so well, how could rulers make peasants grow crops that "they could not eat, or process to serve local needs?"[23] Indeed, how would global labor be mobilized in an age of freedom? Imperial bureaucrats worked zealously to find ways to reconstruct the worldwide web of cotton production, including what, in the United States, has come to be known as Reconstruction.

Postwar cotton growing can be seen as an example of the global nature of social conflict involving rural cultivators, merchants, imperial statesmen, landowners, and industrialists. Although the specific outcome of this conflict differed from one region of the world to another, the broad contours of the labor system that emerged in cotton growing were similar: nowhere in the world were workers re-enslaved. At the same time, the desire of many rural cultivators, especially in the Southern United States, to turn themselves into landowning farmers who would be able to choose subsistence production over cotton-for-export also failed. Instead, a system of sharecropping and tenant farming evolved, in which cotton growers owned themselves and, sometimes, their tools and, drawing on metropolitan capital, grew cotton for world markets.

In the Southern United States, when efforts failed to turn former slaves into ill-paid wage workers laboring in gangs, sharecropping emerged as an economic compromise secured by a wide variety of laws passed by legislatures that were, in turn, controlled by planters' representatives. Sharecropping gave cultivators a modicum of control over their labor, while keeping them landless. From the perspective of landowners, sharecropping enabled them to retain control over labor and land. This reconstruction of cotton regimes in the US South was informed by and in turn informed such reconstructions of the global cotton-growing countryside elsewhere, from India to western Africa. And that reconstruction of cotton agriculture also allowed the US South to remain an important cotton producer for world markets, even though Southern growers now found themselves in competition with producers in other parts of the world, such as India and Egypt, who had gotten their start during the Civil War and were exerting downward pressure on global cotton prices. Southern producers who had benefited from the largely undifferentiated market in cotton—due to the phenomenal output of the slave-based plantation complex, a compliant state, and unparalleled access to financial credit—now faced rigorous international competition.

Cotton Textiles

During the last decades of the nineteenth century, the South moved beyond cotton farming into the business of cotton textile production. The American South was, in fact, at the vanguard of a global movement that saw the world's cotton industry shift to lower-wage locations. The massive relocation of the cotton industry into the Southern United States had its start at the International Cotton Exposition of 1881 in Atlanta. There, cotton machinery displayed as the *Exposition*

Cotton Mills afterward became a functioning mill. What followed was growth so fast that by 1910 the American South was the world's third-largest producer of cotton thread, after Great Britain and the Northern states of the Union. This was an amazing development since at the end of the Civil War there had been hardly any significant cotton manufacturing in the states of the former Confederacy, and as late as 1879 there were seventeen times as many spindles in the North as in the South. By 1919, Southern manufacturers operated 14 million spindles, nearly as many as the 17.5 million spindles turning in the Northern states at that time.[24]

Geography—particularly, proximity to cotton fields—played less of a role in this sudden expansion of cotton manufacturing in the US South than might be expected. Indeed, the slightly lower costs of accessing cotton were offset by the cost of shipping finished goods to Northern markets. The secret of success was plentiful and cheap labor, or, as economist Elijah Helm put it in 1903, "the excessively low labor cost." The destruction of slavery and the attendant transformation of the countryside had created a large and malleable pool of low-wage workers for the cotton factories—at first mostly white rural workers who had once been tenant farmers and, later, African American workers, most of them former sharecroppers. As one contemporary observed, Southern cotton growers left the farms "like rats leaving a sinking ship."[25]

Endowed, thus, with huge supplies of cheap labor and aided by supportive local and regional governments, budding local Northern manufacturers opened additional mills in short order. Many of these operations were financed by selling stock to local communities and by securing loans from Northern machine makers seeking markets for their equipment. At the same time lax labor laws, low taxes, low wages, and the absence of trade unions made the South alluring to cotton manufacturers. It was a region of the United States "where the labor agitator is not such a power, and where the manufacturers are not constantly harassed by new and nagging restrictions." As the editor of the *Lynchburg News* put it in 1895, Northern manufacturers moved their milling operations south in an effort "to get away from the meddlesome and restrictive laws enacted at the instigation of 'walking delegates' and lazy agitators."[26]

Low wages characterized these operations, wages depressed in large part because cotton mills could draw on a large number of very young and very cheap workers. In 1905, 23 percent of all workers in Southern cotton mills were younger than sixteen, compared to only 6 percent in the Northern states. Thanks to the absence of national standards, people also worked longer hours in the South—sixty-four hours per week, or even seventy-five hours, were not uncommon. In fact, cotton industrialists' influence over Southern state governments—and the disenfranchisement of large segments of the local working class, especially, but not only, African Americans, that began during the 1880s—allowed for much laxer labor laws than in other states of the union, a defining characteristic of emerging cotton industries throughout the global South. Cotton industrialization, moreover, had strong backing from state governments, whose legislators and governors were vulnerable to the enormous influence and power of organized industrialists.[27]

The American South remained important to the global cotton economy just as cotton continued to be important to the South throughout the nineteenth century. By 1910, the cotton-manufacturing industry of the US South was booming, and the states of the former Confederacy were still, by far, the most important suppliers of raw cotton to global markets. Yet the South's forms of integration had changed. It had morphed from the world's most important producer of raw cotton by slave labor for European factories to a cotton-manufacturing power in its own right based on cheap, but nonbonded, labor, while at the same time still supplying the lion's share of the world cotton industry's raw material, thanks to the labor of millions of sharecroppers and tenant farmers.

A Laboratory of Global Capitalism

The American South—through its relationship with cotton—can be viewed as a giant laboratory of global capitalism. It was not, contrary to many assertions, a backwater of the Industrial Revolution, but instead it was at its very forefront, the location of some of the era's most significant social and economic transformations. Slaveholders and regional commentators considered cotton and slavery to be "structural strengths," and they rejected any fatalistic assumptions that the regional economy faced long-term doom. To be sure, its own industrialization had to await the abolition of slavery and therefore lagged behind other areas of the world, yet the American South was in the vanguard when it came to linking the global Industrial Revolution to the vast expansion of slavery. The American South also showed how the global countryside could be transformed in the wake of slavery's abolition, remaining throughout the nineteenth century at the forefront when it came to the *mise en valeur* (make economically useful) of recently captured territories, setting an example for many European colonialists in Africa and Asia to aspire to with varying degrees of success. And the industrialization of the American South showed the way for the expansion of industry throughout the Global South that would unfold throughout the twentieth century.[28]

This vanguard role of the American South was partly the result of its peculiar political and economic character, which made it both strange and unique. The distinctiveness of the American South in the larger history of the expansion of capitalism was most fundamentally the result of its incorporation into a highly complex polity—the United States of America. Unlike other slave regions of the world, Brazil and the Caribbean among them, the American South was embedded in a nation-state that also contained territories in which people embraced very different ideas, institutions, and political economies. In Massachusetts and New York, in Pennsylvania and Illinois, the order of the day throughout most of the nineteenth century had been the building of an expansive industrial economy, with protected markets, wage labor, and a state committed to the political economy of domestic industrialization. How to incorporate a post–Civil War South into this political economy would stamp the United States in decisive ways to this day, as this conflict left behind a legacy of deep political divisions, splintered labor markets, and racism.

RICHARD FOLLETT

The Rise and Fall of
American Sugar

❧

SUGAR WAS NOT the most important crop in the American South, but it defined the history of the Atlantic world. No other agricultural commodity was so intimately linked to the rise of slavery as cane sugar. From the fifteenth to the nineteenth centuries, slavery and sugar lay at the axis of international capitalism. The colonial plantation system reached its apogee by the mid-eighteenth century. Hundreds of thousands of enslaved Africans toiled on estates from Brazil to the Caribbean producing sugar for export. The profits greased the wheels of Atlantic commerce, enlarging bankers, shippers, and planters on both sides of the ocean, while the voracious demand for enslaved laborers fueled the expansion of the Atlantic slave trade. A triangular network of slaves, sugar, and manufactured goods circulated around the Atlantic basin, feeding the plantation complex with labor and the Europeans with the sucrose they craved. Once a luxury commodity, sugar was a staple of European diets by 1800, and its consumption drove one of the largest and earliest mass markets in world history. Indeed, its history was as important to the eighteenth century as cotton's was to the nineteenth. The United States entered the sugar trade as a relative latecomer. Louisiana, however, made up for lost time. It was the last of the New World sugar colonies, and, like its competitors in the Caribbean, Louisiana bound its fate to slavery and the plantation system.[1]

By 1900, the New World sugar colonies had lost their pivotal role.

The once lucrative tropical plantation societies no longer dominated the world sugar markets, and the nineteenth-century global economy proved hostile to the political economy of sugar and slavery. Geopolitical shifts toward the temperate Northern and Southern Hemispheres eliminated the primacy of the colonial tropics. Capital, immigrants, and trade flowed to settler societies in North America, Australia, South Africa, and Argentina. By contrast, the "old" eighteenth-century sugar colonies appeared to be falling behind. They were not part of the great divergence by which Britain and the Western economies outpaced the rest of the world, and they failed to exhibit the same type of protean energy that James Belich describes for other Anglophone and settler societies across the globe. Furthermore, the shift from merchant capitalism to industrial capitalism (from trade- and exchange-based capitalism to wage labor– and manufacturing-based capitalism) proved particularly harmful to tropical societies that flourished under mercantilism. Slavery deprived plantation societies of the capital required for industrial modernity, ensuring that wherever slavery lingered progress halted. The tropical New World was peripheral to the ascendant age of industrial capitalism, and its commercial hubs beat to a slower, more inefficient rhythm than those of the industrial Atlantic.[2]

The abolition of slavery unleashed colossal change throughout plantation America, but it did not bring the plantation system to an end. Throughout tropical America, cane sugar farming remained land extensive and labor intensive with coercive labor practices dominating the plantation mode of production. Planters attempted to meet these labor needs by implementing wage-labor contracts or apprenticeship schemes or by recruiting laborers from low-income nations, specifically India and China. European nation-states smoothed the new traffic in humans, but the labor experiments failed to supplant black workers from the New World sugar fields. Sharecropping, the dominant labor system of American cotton after emancipation, made little headway in the tropics (at least initially). The diverse rural settlement pattern of tenant farming likewise faltered as landlords from the Brazilian lowlands to the Mississippi River reinforced patronage,

paternalism, and dependent class relations over the families of mar-
ginalized cane workers who continued to reside in plantation villages,
much as they had done under slavery.[3]

Tropical producers, however, faced a global market for their commodities and a hostile political environment. Antislavery and free trade
advanced in tandem, eliminating protective tariffs and the assured imperial structures under which New World sugar rose to prominence.
The free circulation of cheap sugar presented almost insurmountable
challenges for aristocratic planters in the original sugar colonies. In
turn, British, French, and American regimes oversaw the expansion of
new sugar industries in Asia, Africa, and the Pacific. Cane growers in
India, Mauritius (an island nation in the Indian Ocean), South Africa,
Java, Fiji, Australia, the Philippines, and Hawaii ramped up production,
harvesting eight-feet-tall canes, extracting the sugar juice, and then
evaporating it—in manufacturing facilities—to produce refined sugar.
As much an industry as an agricultural enterprise, the sugar complex
also extended across the Americas with Argentine, Peruvian, and US
farmers in Florida and Texas all contributing to the global sugar market
from the 1890s. Improved cane breeds developed at international research stations further enabled sugar farming to expand toward the
close of the nineteenth century. European-based sugar beets, however,
represented the greatest challenge to the primacy of tropical sugar.
Grown like potatoes, with the sugar coming from the tuber, beets revolutionized the geography of world sugar. By the mid-nineteenth century, sugar beet farming surged, particularly in France and Germany,
and by the early 1880s beet sugar production outstripped cane. Consumers proved to be the chief beneficiaries of cheap sugars, but tropical
producers in the old sugar colonies found the competition and declining prices ruinous.[4] Like their American compatriots in the rice industry, New World sugar producers faced a vast undifferentiated world
market filled with cheap and virtually indistinguishable sugars. It was
commodity hell—part two.

By the eve of the First World War, the tropical plantation system and
its regimen of coerced, dependent labor crumbled as quickly as the
chimney-stack on a dilapidated boiling house. Unable to compete in a

global sugar market—where free trade, not protectionism, dominated—New World sugar producers faced decades of gradual decline. Huge sugar producers in Cuba and Puerto Rico weathered the storms of global trade, but American cane farmers struggled to survive. In less than a century, they had experienced the rise and fall of the plantation complex and the highs and lows of international trade as Louisiana sugar surged forward under slavery, only to collapse in the era of free labor and free trade. As historical geographer J. R. Galloway observes, the nineteenth century represented a "period of crisis" for the New World sugar colonies. None of them retained the privileged trade position they enjoyed in 1800, nor did they enjoy a monopoly over governments, labor, or maritime power. A century later, decaying plantation houses along the banks of the Mississippi told a story of monumental decline. Yet the rise and fall of American sugar was not just a story of regional failure. Far from it—Louisiana's past encapsulates the history of tropical America. There, the plantation system rose and fell, slavery gave way to freedom, and commercial protection collapsed with global free trade. To be sure, coercive labor relations endured, but Louisiana's sugar planters—like their landed neighbors in the American rice swamps—faced a long road to economic perdition.[5]

America's Sugar Kingdom

The United States was a late arrival in the world sugar market. Before the 1790s, practically no sugar cane was raised in continental North America. French settlers in colonial New Orleans began experimenting with cane in the 1750s, though these first attempts seldom proved successful. With Saint-Domingue sugar production booming, neither French nor Spanish authorities devoted much attention to Louisiana or its agricultural potential. Their inattention was well founded. On the eve of the French Revolution, Saint-Domingue dominated world sugar production. Enslaved laborers produced almost seventy-nine thousand tons of sugar in 1791 alone. Rich and prosperous, the French colony, Moreau de Saint-Méry wrote, "takes on air of opulence that dazzles

Europeans." Against these figures and such affluence, attempts in Louisiana to produce a single pound of sugar appeared risible. The 1791 crop was the largest yet on Saint-Domingue and the last to be produced by slave labor. That August, slaves in the northern part of the island rose in revolt, finally securing their freedom and the political independence of Haiti in January 1804. Sugar production ground to a halt. The plantation system collapsed, and in contrast to the rest of the Caribbean, where forced labor shaped the history of emancipation, Haitians turned to small-scale semisubsistence agriculture. Sugar production never recovered, and by 1825 Haitian farmers manufactured just one ton of sugar. This dramatic collapse presented a formidable economic opportunity for cane growers elsewhere in the Caribbean. Practically every colonial state increased production, including French and Spanish Louisiana, where the arrival of émigré planters from Saint-Domingue helped foster a small sugar cane industry. Other French- and Creole-born planters, including Étienne de Boré, were among the first to granulate Louisiana sugar. Boré was not exactly the "savior of Louisiana," as the nineteenth-century historian Charles Gayarré declared, though his sugar works helped transform the lower Mississippi valley from a "rogue colony" into a "slave country," to cite two recent historians of colonial and early national Louisiana.[6]

Boré's success, however, stemmed from his use of innovative techniques for both cultivation and irrigation. As French explorer Georges Collot observed, by the turn of the eighteenth century, the small, though budding, industry lay in the hands of "great colonial capitalists," about fifty of whom produced sugar along the lower reaches of the Mississippi River. Cane farming swiftly expanded beyond the New Orleans hinterland, and, on the eve of the US acquisition of Louisiana, a sugar plantation complex emerged under the command of leading Francophone and Creole families. Each sugar estate produced on average 120,000 pounds of raw brown sugar from one hundred French arpents (roughly eighty-five acres) of cane land, with slave crews numbering forty. Approximately seventy-five sugar estates operated in the first years of the nineteenth century, the largest manufacturing

200,000 pounds of sugar. Although subsequent production engulfed that of the early planters, the Louisiana crop of 1802 already valued $850,000, much of which was sold in the United States.[7]

The Louisiana Purchase (1803) unlocked the market opportunities of duty-free trade with the rest of the United States. Louisianans seized the opportunity, and by 1812, when Louisiana formally entered the Union, sugar production expanded in scale and scope. The familiar processes of the plantation revolution, moreover, were visibly underway. W. C. C. Claiborne, Louisiana's first territorial governor, noted as early as 1806 that the "facility with which sugar planters amass wealth is almost incredible." Planters had doubled the value of their estates within three years and began a process of land consolidation and monopolization. They occupied the best land along the Mississippi, and by 1811 one observer recorded that "there are but few of the petty habitants, the lands being engrossed by the wealthy planters." With smallholders edged out of the industry, planters multiplied their investment in racial slavery, converting the rich alluvial bottomlands into slave societies where the enslaved population soon dwarfed the free. By 1820, the rural parishes lying upriver from New Orleans were fully immersed in the plantation revolution. Three-quarters of the population of St. Charles Parish was enslaved; slaves represented a numerical majority in neighboring St. John the Baptist and St. James Parishes, while other explosive signals of plantation slavery emerged. On January 8, 1811, the largest slave revolt in American history took place on the German Coast, some thirty-five miles north of New Orleans. Five hundred slaves, armed with their cane knives, marched on New Orleans, burning plantations before a federal force suppressed the uprising. Planters responded swiftly and abruptly to the revolt, revealing their "characteristic barbarity," one observer recalled. Decapitating the rebel leaders, slaveholders displayed the severed heads on poles along the banks of the Mississippi. It was an ominous warning to those who challenged the hegemony of sugar and slavery.[8]

The arrival of land-thirsty American settlers in the aftermath of the War of 1812 accelerated the process of land consolidation, slave investment, and the monocultivation of sugar. Buoyed by the federal protection of domestic US sugar, American settlers were "swarming in," one French traveler reported, each one with a "little plan of speculation." They were, it seemed, invading Louisiana as "the holy tribes once swarmed over the land of Canaan." Francis DuBose Richardson, who emigrated—like many of his class—from Virginia to Louisiana in the 1830s recalled that Anglo-American planters were "rushing to the sugar gold fields, each with his own idea of working them to his best advantage." Converting "waste lands into verdant fields," settlers reaped "stores of gold and silver from the glebe they turned up." The bounteous harvests, however, owed their profitability to federal tariff protection. Nurtured from the dangers of free trade, Louisiana cane producers benefited substantially from the federal duty of 2.5 cents per pound levied on foreign sugars. With this duty as an effective buffer against foreign competition and the domestic market assured, planters eagerly turned to sugar. Cane farming, moreover, proved hugely profitable. Planters whose production costs ranged from 4 to 4.5 cents per pound received between 6 and 8 cents per pound for their domestic Louisiana sugar in the 1820s. Sugar prices fluctuated though they remained essentially stable throughout the second decade of the nineteenth century. By contrast, cotton growers watched the price of their staple decline by as much as a third during the 1820s. With low prospects for cotton, "every landholder grasps with avidity," William Darby wrote, "at a prospect of changing his cotton into sugar lands."[9]

Boosted by federal protection and depressed cotton prices, the frontier of Louisiana sugar production expanded beyond its initial core into the agricultural hinterland. Cane cultivation extended west to the bayous and rivers that bisected the Atchafalaya Basin and stretched along the Mississippi, past Baton Rouge, toward the old French colonial outpost of Pointe Coupee. The number of sugar estates grew in tandem. In 1824, 193 sugar plantations operated in the state; by 1830, this number had more than trebled to 691. Finally, the enslaved population grew swiftly with the plantation revolution. St. James Parish, located near the epicenter of the colonial and early national sugar industry saw its enslaved population increase two and a half times from 1810 to 1830; it trebled in Ascension Parish, located midway between Baton Rouge and New Orleans, and grew fourfold along the banks of Bayou Lafourche to the west of the Mississippi. Wherever present, sugar wove its distinct demographic signature. Practically every sugar parish had a substantial black majority; in some places the enslaved population outstripped whites four to one. Men also outnumbered women, on some plantations by a ratio of five to three, and these slaves proved particularly youthful. Slave traders fed the voracious demand for human capital, supplying the New Orleans slave markets with single males, typically aged seventeen to twenty-five. These young, strong enslaved men formed the backbone of Louisiana's sugar revolution.[10]

Like its competitors in the Spanish Caribbean, Louisiana's sugar interests danced to the tune of international and domestic sugar markets. Nineteenth-century demand for sucrose rose sharply, in no small measure because of its relative affordability. By 1831, every American consumed thirteen pounds of sugar per annum, while a decade later most adults consumed eighteen pounds annually. By midcentury, consumption surpassed thirty pounds. Only the British retained a sweeter tooth than the Americans, ensuring that the domestic American market proved large and invaluable to producers, be they domestic or foreign. By midcentury, the annual demand for sucrose approached nine hundred million pounds, a fourfold increase in twenty years. The American fixation with sugar, the trade journal *Hunt's Merchants Magazine* declared, reflected the "improved prosperity of the United States." Per capita income among the nation's free population rose from $109 to $144 between 1840 and 1860, an increase of more than 30 percent. Domestic sugar prices oscillated over the same period, but declined by 1.5 cents per pound from the 1820s to the Civil War. Equipped with greater personal income, many Americans could afford ever cheapening sugar and paid handsomely for it, even when prices surged in 1844, 1847, and most particularly during 1856 and 1857. Even among common laborers, sugar proved relatively affordable, with a pound of sugar declining from 16–17 percent of the daily wage in the 1820s to 6–9 percent by the 1850s. Sugar's transition from eighteenth-century luxury to nineteenth-century staple provided a lucrative domestic market for Louisiana's cane planters, but their future would inevitably be shaped by their capacity (or incapacity) to meet US demand.[11]

There were, however, limits to growth. First, sugar is a forced crop in Louisiana. Until the introduction of modern frost-resistant canes, cane farming on the lower reaches of the Mississippi proved a perilous pursuit. Located on the northern rim of the Caribbean sugar-producing belt, Louisiana faced a series of overlapping meteorological problems. Icy winds from the upper Midwest swept down the nation's central corridor, bringing sharp frosts that froze the sucrose-rich juice within the canes and rendered it all but worthless. Cane growers faced an almost impossible dilemma—they could plant the majority of their seed crop in January and harvest the six- to eight-foot-tall canes some nine or ten months later. But, in doing so, the work crews who entered the fields in mid- to late October harvested immature cane with lower sucrose content than that enjoyed by their Caribbean rivals. Alternatively, they could wait a few weeks more, maturing their canes, but pitting their fortunes against the climes. Whether they gambled or not, cane farmers recognized that cane required a growing season of 250 frost-free days, mean temperatures in the mid-70s Fahrenheit, and approximately fifty inches of rain per annum. Humid, subtropical southern Louisiana met these criteria, but the warming effect of the Gulf of Mexico declined swiftly, ensuring that cane could not be commercially farmed in most parts of the South. Planters along the Atlantic coast experimented with cane in Georgia and South Carolina in the 1820s, but these attempts proved in vain. Although newer, hardier, and more rapidly maturing cane varieties, notably Ribbon cane, replaced the older and frost-susceptible Creole and Otaheite varieties in the 1830s, even these innovations failed to expand the sugar production zone substantially. By the eve of the Civil War, then, cane farming dominated southern Louisiana with small satellite industries emerging in northeastern Florida and in southern Texas. For the rest of the nineteenth century, these three states dominated continental US cane production, with Louisiana remaining firmly at the vanguard.[12]

If American sugar cane was climatically confined, it remained (like rice) spatially limited too. Louisiana's alluvial landscape provided plenty of rich soil, but much of it remained flooded or waterlogged. Rivers snaked through the landscape, often spilling into marshland or swamp. The bayous and rivers, however, formed natural levees above the water line. These levee crests were better drained than the neighboring backswamp and more suitable for cane cultivation. Sugar plantations thus hugged the river crests, with mills and plantation houses erected either directly on the levee front or just to the rear. Since rivers also served as the principal, indeed almost sole, means to transport sugar to market until the 1850s, planters privileged navigable access, and the typical sugar plantation featured narrow river frontage, prized levee soils, and backswamp. This regional topography lent a distinctive character to landholding and settlement patterns within the sugar country. From the air, the sugar country appeared as a network of alluvial corridors featuring long, thin estates that began on the river crest and petered out in the dank backswamps. Despite these environmental difficulties, cane growers in the region remained relatively sanguine, confidently predicting that Louisiana, aided by Florida and Texas, would soon furnish enough sugar to "meet all the demands" of the entire US domestic market.[13]

Having established the plantation complex by 1830, cane planters expanded operations in the 1840s. Once again, federal tariff protection and depressed cotton prices played instrumental roles, with changing federal administrations whistling different tunes when it came to American trade policy. The 1842 protectionist tariff, introduced by the congressional Whigs, restored the 2.5 cent duty on imported brown sugars, ensuring that local prices advanced to profitable levels. By contrast, cotton prices remained relatively low. With these factors in mind, planters who had previously grown cotton—during the flush times of the 1830s—switched to cane cultivation. Moreover, the hardier ribbon variety enabled cotton planters in central portions of the state to convert to sugar or open new estates on land previously considered unsuitable for cane. In effect, the sugar industry operated as a foil to the cotton revolution, with the number of sugar estates expanding when cotton prospects dipped or when protectionist tariffs promised good returns. The number of sugar estates accordingly increased to 1,500 by midcentury, with cane grown along central Louisiana's Red River. Baton Rouge, the *American Agriculturist* announced, was fast becoming the "central point" of America's sugar kingdom, with cane grown deep into the interior: "[s]uch has been the success of the last two years that many new mills are being erected, and vast quantities of land brought into cultivation in places where it would have been thought madness to talk of making sugar ten years ago." Sugar plantations were also more productive. In 1830, the average sugar estate produced 108 hogsheads (a container of sugar roughly weighing 1,000 pounds); by 1844, this figure increased to 269 hogsheads, and, in the bumper 1853 crop, each estate averaged more than 310 hogsheads. Sugar production thus grew in scale and scope. The 1846 Walker tariff, however, slammed the regional economy into reverse, with its impact most keenly felt among small and medium-sized cane producers. President James K. Polk's Democratic administration sought to lower tariffs, open the domestic market, and embrace free trade. Led by Southern cotton planters eager for cheap manufactured goods, Democrats slashed the Whig's so-called "Black" protectionist tariffs. Sugar growers soon felt the effect. The Walker measure reduced sugar's tariff protection to 30 percent ad valorem; this rate continued until 1857 when Congress lowered it to 24 percent. Under these rates, the average duty on sugar equated to 1.11 cents per pound, a reduction in half from the earlier Whig tariff. Oscillating federal policies swiftly came home to roost. During the 1850s when protectionism collapsed and cotton prices recovered, the number of sugar estates declined to 1,300 as farmers—particularly on the northern edge of the sugar belt—returned to the safety of cotton. Those who left the industry, moreover, tended to be smaller, marginal sugar producers, ensuring that while the absolute number of sugar farmers declined, the industry remained firmly in the hands of large operators with vast slave crews. By the close of the antebellum era, large sugar planters owned on average 110 slaves, 1,600 acres of land, and produced 500–600 hogsheads of sugar per estate.[14]

Under the leadership of this rural elite, the domestic sugar industry nevertheless expanded production sharply. Mean annual production rose from 74,000 hogsheads in the 1830s to 165,000 hogsheads in the 1840s before rising again to 275,000 in the 1850s. Two additional steps, however, proved central to the transformation and acceleration of Louisiana's plantation revolution. First, with relatively accessible credit and federal protection, planters tapped the domestic slave trade for young, strong men, upon which sugar production rested. The number of slaves cultivating sugar rose sharply from 21,000 in 1827 to 65,000 in 1844, before surpassing 125,000 by midcentury. The average plantation workforce increased from 52 in 1830 to roughly 85 in 1850, although many of the biggest estates featured slave workforces 150 strong. Second, planters also invested heavily in technology, replacing their old animal-powered sugar mills with semi-industrial steam-driven facilities.[15]

Steam-powered three-roller mills increased sugar extraction rates from 50 percent in animal-powered mills to 80 percent in a steam mill. The new technology, moreover, enabled planters to increase the acreage under crop, confident that when the harvest came they could grind the cane swiftly. Introduced in 1822, steam-powered sugar mills crushed the new varietals of ribbon cane with greater ease, but at $12,000 the price of a mill proved prohibitive for anyone save a small minority of the wealthiest elite. By the 1830s, steam power had been harnessed in multiple ways (notably on steamboats), and the price of a domestically built steam-driven sugar mill had fallen by half. The affordability of steam-powered technology—buoyed by a lucrative secondhand market in steam engines—ensured its widespread application, and the number of estates incorporating steam power increased fourfold from 1828 to 1841. By 1850, more than nine hundred plantations featured steam power; they produced practically all of the state's commercial cane crop, while those who retained animal-powered mills found themselves isolated on the geographic and productive margins of the industry. Those who plowed ahead with the steam revolution enjoyed production gains and advantages accrued by economies of scale. The number of acres cultivated per hand almost doubled in the antebellum decades, while the average yield of sugar per hand also increased to seven hogsheads, a two- to threefold increase over early nineteenth-century West Indian estates and a figure matched only by the most productive Cuban plantations.[16]

Most planters by midcentury had grasped the technical panacea of steam, though the same planters who oversaw the steam revolution proved slow converts to the hugely expensive vacuum processing facilities that appeared in the 1850s—but which were not fully adopted by Louisiana planters until the postbellum era. These multiple-effect evaporators used the heat generated by the exhaust of a steam engine, rather than the direct heat of a furnace, to reduce the sugar juice to granulation point. The earliest vacuum pans dated to the mid-1810s, though they were substantially advanced by French engineers Louis-Charles Derosne and Jean-François Cail, who developed a series of evaporating pans that employed the principle of latent heat. In Louisiana, Norbert Rillieux—a free person of color in New Orleans—patented his multiple-effect vacuum pans in 1843. The use of steam vacuums minimized the risk of scorching or discoloring the sugar and produced a higher-grade, whiter sugar than the standard plantation grade produced by open kettles.

By 1846, a small group of planters, numbering no more than thirty, had adopted one of the different vacuum techniques. The high price of fancy-grade sugar and the enhanced 1842 tariff proved instrumental in fueling confidence among the very wealthy who sought to benefit from the 6 cent import duty paid on white and powdered sugars. Plantation-grade raw sugar, by contrast, retained only a 2.5 cent rate. Consequently, the 1842 tariff had a disproportionate, pump-priming effect on the sugar elite who invested up to $30,000 to acquire a multiple effect evaporator. The price tag was high, too high in fact for most planters, who continued to produce sugar in open kettles, clarifying and evaporating the sugar juice in a set (or train) of pans. Reservations also abounded as to whether the Rillieux apparatus was "too complicated to be entrusted" to African Americans. Concerns over the compatibility of advanced technology with black labor troubled planters throughout much of the nineteenth century. In the antebellum era, however, the cost of vacuum processing ensured that this remained a relatively moot point. Some planters experimented with partnerships and mergers to enhance their capital bases, but even these lacked the financial liquidity to advance the industry substantially.[17]

To compel enslaved people to labor at the metered cadence of the steam age, slaveholders redoubled their commitment to drilled gang labor. Long hours, grueling work regimes, and brutal corporal punishment had long characterized New World slavery, above all on sugar estates. As James Ramsey observed of the eighteenth-century West Indies, "[T]he discipline of a sugar plantation is exact as a regiment." And so it remained. The annual harvest season was a rush against time, as slaves worked feverishly to process the canes into sugar at double-quick speed. In Louisiana, this proved to be an absolute necessity because of the dangers of frost damage and the short harvest season in the state. Elsewhere in the sugar world, speed remained important. Sugar cane is a perishable commodity, and it must be processed quickly (ideally within twenty-four hours) after it is cut. The problem of biodeterioration had bedeviled cane planters for centuries. Steam power increased processing speed, but even the biggest mill turned slowly if its cane supply proved erratic. Louisiana's sugar masters addressed this disjuncture directly. They dragooned slave laborers and synchronized field operations with those in the millhouse. Slaveholders used the whip liberally and introduced financial incentives to compel and cajole slaves to toil through the night. These ancient practices and management innovations had enduring significance, but they enabled planters to introduce a fully industrialized stage to the plantation revolution.[18]

America's sugar revolution, however, took place in an era of global market integration. Capital, credit, and commodities assumed standardized forms as the ethics of exchange bound riverfront farms in Louisiana with the urban hubs of nineteenth-century industrialization, London, New York, and Paris. Slavery was itself transformed by the intersection of capitalism, forced labor, and international commerce. Indeed, so substantial were these transformations that historians would do well to adopt Dale Tomich's formulation of "second slavery" to capture the step change in market integration, systematic redeployment of capital, and expansion of slavery in the nineteenth

century. Racial bondage—however repugnant to our modern values—
was not an archaic institution incompatible with modernity. Tragically for those in chains, antebellum slavery was highly adaptable, de-
livering vast profits to those in the plantation mansions. Rational
(including risk-averse) business practices prevailed, enslaved people
were forcibly transformed into productive plantation machines, a
bourgeois middle class flourished in the slave states, and its wealthiest citizens thrived as part of the global economic order.[19]

But, for all their apparent symbols of economic progress, planters
found the world sugar market to be an increasingly uncomfortable
place. From 1837 to 1858, Louisiana's cane belt supplied 46 percent of
domestic sugar demand. On occasion, notably in the mid-1840s, Louisiana farmers produced more than 60 percent of the national demand,
but, as sugar consumption rose steeply in the 1850s, the domestic
sugar industry struggled to maintain its market share from its relatively limited agricultural lands. Poor domestic crops in the mid- to
late 1850s forced sugar brokers to rely even more extensively on Caribbean imports as Louisianans nervously watched Cuban and Puerto
Rican sugars arrive on New York and Philadelphia wharves in increasing volume. The scale of Spanish-Caribbean imports escalated swiftly,
particularly those of Cuba. In 1840, for instance, Cubans exported almost 50 million pounds of sugar to the United States; a decade later
this figure had surpassed 125 million pounds, and during the 1850s
Havana- and New York–based shippers conducted a flourishing trade.
In 1851 alone, longshoremen working on the Hudson and East Rivers
unloaded 94,000 hogsheads and 188,000 boxes (each containing four
hundred pounds) of sugar from Cuba. Six years later, some 150,000
Cuban hogsheads were received in Manhattan, and, on New Year's Eve
1860, officials at the Port of New York calculated that 230,000 hogsheads and 165,000 boxes of Cuban sugar had arrived during the calendar year, a grand total of almost 150,000 tons or 300 million pounds of
sugar. Added to that lay another 22,000 tons of Puerto Rican sugar that
waterfront workers unloaded onto New York's crowded quays. Louisiana's entire crop of 228,000 hogsheads (approximately 228 million
pounds) simply could not match the volume of imported Caribbean

sugars that stevedores and draymen along the Atlantic seaboard heaved onto carts bound for warehouses and sugar refineries.[20]

In reality and as Louisiana's planters well understood, only the maintenance of federal tariff protection ensured profits. The tariff was "a question of life and death with us in Louisiana," planter Alexander Porter proclaimed. But for many outside observers, the tariff cocooned sugar planters from market competition and artificially kept the price of imported sugars above the domestic article. Ordinary Americans appeared to be paying elevated prices merely to benefit a rural slaveholding aristocracy. Louisiana's sugar elite countered these accusations, stating that the higher operating costs in Louisiana—compared to those enjoyed by West Indian producers—ensured that sugar could be profitably made only for 5.5 cents, whereas Caribbean sugar returned a profit at 3 cents a pound. Tariff protection, they argued, provided an indispensable shield against the volatility of the world market, but, as the nation descended into civil war, US producers had reason to cheer. The bumper 1861 harvest was the largest sugar crop on record and the crowning moment of the antebellum sugar masters. It was also the last crop to be made entirely with enslaved labor.[21]

American Sugar Empire

The Civil War unleashed revolutionary change within American society. Slave emancipation liberated 4 million men and women from bondage (including some 125,000 in the sugar country). In contrast to the British Caribbean, where slaveholders received financial compensation to liberate their human property, emancipation wiped millions of dollars from the portfolios of the South's wealthiest planters. Lincoln's wartime policies, moreover, shifted the locus of national wealth creation firmly toward the Northeast and Midwest, while the growth of the federal state fundamentally weakened the autonomy and political economy of the planter class. Louisiana's sugar interests were hit hard. By 1865, sugar production slumped to levels not known since the 1790s and fewer than two hundred plantations remained in operation, while the value of Louisiana's sugar industry collapsed sevenfold. Louisiana's plantation complex, however, was not entirely shattered. Federal troops occupied much of the antebellum sugar country from April 1862 and General Nathaniel Banks's labor system established a halfway house between slavery and freedom. In return for wages (paid in cash individually or collectively as one-twentieth of the crop), field workers resided on sugar estates and labored in gangs much as they had done previously. Union occupation thus buttressed the plantation system and the stable labor units planters needed, particularly as harvest approached. This backward compromise set the tone for postemancipation labor relations in the sugar country. Plantation agriculture endured, freedpeople continued to live in old slave cabins, and massed gang labor continued, albeit with workers now receiving cash wages for their labor. This new arrangement also ensured that while sharecropping emerged as the predominant labor system in most of the cotton South, a waged proletariat underpinned the plantation economy in the American cane world. Louisiana planters were not alone in adopting this solution. In postemancipation Jamaica, sugar planters sought to restrict the liberties enjoyed by former slaves, implementing apprenticeship programs whereby former slaves labored on the plantations for low wages. These "bungled efforts to gain greater control" over the labor force, historian Thomas Holt observes, only exacerbated the freedpeople's desire to flee the sugar estates. Louisiana's planters also discovered that their former slaves wished to put freedom into practice by halting work to attend political meetings, striking for higher wages, and walking off the job. Women, in particular, withdrew from the plantation order, while estate managers complained vociferously about former slaves absconding or, as they disapprovingly called it, "skulking about."[22]

With less than 10 percent of planters able to recruit (or keep) a full complement of African American workers by 1869, interest turned to foreign labor. As former slaveholders lamented, the "labor problem" might be resolved by the recruitment of Chinese laborers. Asian workers, planters believed, would "labor faithfully and satisfactorily" in the cane fields. As the *Louisiana Sugar Bowl* observed, the "Chinaman" was "so much like the old Sambo and could be worked on the gang order." These assumptions were not entirely without logic. The young, strong Chinese workers conformed to the gender- and musculature-defined notions of the idealized sugar worker, and evidence from the Cuban sugar industry suggested that "coolies" and cane worked well. Moreover, coolies—planters believed—could be bossed in ways reminiscent of slavery. Between 1847 and 1873, more than 120,000 Chinese workers arrived in Cuba, bound for the sugar fields. Elsewhere, colonial officials trafficked Chinese and Indian workers to the British West Indies as a replacement for enslaved labor. The international search for labor was a desperate attempt on the behalf of New World planters to address the apparent scarcity of labor in postemancipation societies, but it was also a conservative step to maintain old structures of labor exploitation and sustain the gang-labor plantation system.[23]

The experiment with immigrant labor on Louisiana's cane estates proved considerably smaller than the contract labor programs of Cuba or Trinidad. Foreign workers from Germany, Scandinavia, Portugal, Ireland, and, above all, southern Italy also toiled in American cane fields alongside Asian workers. Neither group, however, replaced African American workers in Louisiana's cane industry. As one plantation boss bluntly put it, "[T]he feeling among planters is against white laborers and in favor of Negroes because they are used to niggers . . . and a nigger will put up with any kind of fare and for that reason they stick to him like death." Reracializing sugar as a definitively black and male occupation, landlords clung tenaciously to the plantation system and its racial corollary: black labor, white rule. That commitment, however, was tinged with unease. Planters, who had jealously guarded their prewar authority, found the period from 1865 to 1885 particularly vexing. Above all, former slaves leveraged their collective power by striking for higher wages. Since few planters could afford to lose their prime field hands and with few alternative laborers available for hire, strike action proved relatively successful in the late 1870s and 1880s. Planters began to organize in the late 1870s, forming the Louisiana Sugar Planters Association (LSPA), a local, parish-level, and plantation-based organization designed to secure collectively what eluded them privately: authority and control over the cane hands. The organization reduced wages, halted the payment of monthly wages in full, and reverted to the practice of withholding one-third of the cash payment until the close of the harvest. The LSPA was a localized planter-led response to the "labor problem" and a group attempt to reassert the landlords' control over the means of production. These steps advanced still further once white Democratic rule brought the era of Reconstruction to a close in 1877. Newly elected Democrats reinforced the planter class's authority in 1878, founding Louisiana's National Guard as a militarized force to sustain white-line government and the interests of landholders. When cane workers struck in April 1880, armed troops quelled the unrest. Seven years later, after the Knights of Labor orchestrated a series of strikes, planters responded full-bloodedly, calling in the state militia, but only after local vigilantes executed more than thirty cane hands in the aptly named Thibodaux Massacre. As one planter's wife coldly observed, the atrocities in Thibodaux settled "the question of who is to rule: the nigger or the white man? for the next fifty years."[24]

The LSPA's antilabor, antiunion stance did not entirely eliminate workplace strikes, but it severely restricted the mobility of workers. Planters continued to complain about the labor problem and the temporary shortfall of laborers during harvest, though with organized labor effectively crushed in the Louisiana cane fields, strike action virtually ceased from the late 1880s. Plantation managers attempted a further experiment in immigrant labor in the 1890s, recruiting Italian workers for the harvest, but like their earlier trials foreign laborers proved slow and intractable converts to the sugar regime. Despite their intermittent efforts, the solutions to the labor problem offered by the LSPA were local and parochial. By contrast, elsewhere in the sugar world, the colonial state serviced the plantation economy, importing thousands of indentured laborers to work on sugar plantations. Louisiana planters attempted to avail themselves of this international labor supply, but the postwar American state was far from reliable. The 1870 Naturalization Act excluded Asians from citizenship while the 1882 Chinese Exclusion Act restricted the movement of Chinese labor to the United States. By contrast, the European powers harnessed the resources of global empires toward the maintenance and expansion of plantation sugar. Indentured Indian and Chinese workers toiled on cane farms from Peru to Natal (South Africa), and their labor reinforced the social, economic, and historical continuities of global sugar.[25]

If intransigence underpinned the LSPA's attitude toward labor relations, both continuity and change defined its approach to technology. The Civil War triggered severe economic dislocation, including depressed land values, widespread indebtedness, scarce capital, and high rates of interest. Plantations that been valued with all equipment at $200 to $400 an acre in 1850s sold between $35 and $75 an acre by 1870. Sugar production plummeted and did not return to prewar levels until the 1890s. Louisiana's share of the domestic market collapsed to less than 10 percent by 1870. Mechanization advanced sporadically, particularly in field operations, where harvesting cane remained labor intensive. Old working practices endured as did gang labor and the plantation mode. Sugar planters showed little interest in mechanizing field operations, developing cane harvesters, or emulating midwestern wheat and corn growers, who employed mechanical reapers. Yet, despite their grumbles, cane farmers did not challenge the primacy of field labor or substitute their workers for power-driven harvesters. Moreover, it still proved cheaper to hire laborers at a dollar per day for the harvest season than to replace time-worn labor practices with expensive (and unreliable) machinery. Social factors also contributed to the planters' relative conservatism on the question of field labor. Ultimately—and as two generations of historians have shown—landlords remained wedded to the plantation ethos, to regimented labor, and to their authority as both land and labor lords. Gang labor enabled planters to reinforce their racial and class authority, impose direct control over their workers, and perpetuate dependent social relations. The fact that sugar estates continued as residential centers, with cane workers frequently residing in quarters while landlords often lived in the mansions their forefathers constructed, further underscored the sharp dichotomy in power relations. Conservatism thus had its own social and racial utility; progress, by contrast, unsettled the class and racial dominion that landholding planters adhered to.[26]

Planters could not turn back the clock or arrest its forward momentum, however, when it came to the international sugar market. By the last quarter of the nineteenth century, Louisiana sugar was swamped by offshore competition. The introduction of duty-free sugars from Hawaii in 1875 (under a reciprocal trade agreement) presented a direct challenge to Louisiana producers, as did the rise of America's domestic beet sugar industry. The prospects should have been good: domestic sugar consumption increased from thirty-five pounds per capita in 1870 to eighty-three in 1910, but Louisiana's share of the market declined. From 1897 to 1901 cane producers in the continental United States supplied 11 percent of the domestic sugar market. The Hawaiian kingdom—replaced by a pro-US republic in 1894—already supplied more sugar than Louisiana, and, following the US acquisition of Puerto Rico and the Philippines, the annexation of Hawaii (1898), and the introduction of a de facto protectorate over Cuba, thousands of tons of duty-free or reduced-tariff sugar flooded the American market. By 1913, Cuba provided 50 percent of the US domestic sugar market.[27]

Cane sugar in Louisiana began its recovery in the 1880s, though it did not surpass its antebellum peak until 1893. Sugar production in the state, however, consistently surpassed the 300,000 ton threshold during the first decade of the twentieth century. Unfortunately for continental US producers, sugar outputs increased sharply elsewhere, particularly in the Pacific, Asia, and Spanish America. The step change in production was very considerable. In 1850, cane producers throughout the world manufactured approximately 1 million tons of sugar; by 1882, that figured had doubled, and quintupled by 1900. On the eve of the First World War, global cane producers manufactured 10 million tons; by 1941, they neared 20 million tons. Cane sugar production increased not only globally but nationally and provincially too. In 1894, for instance, Cuba topped 1 million tons; the Philippines produced over 330,000 tons the same year; Argentina, which had produced just

30 tons in 1840, manufactured almost 160,000 tons in 1896. The same year cane growers in Java manufactured 500,000 tons, Australian sugar weighed in at 160,000 tons in 1898, and Mauritius punctured the 200,000 ton ceiling in 1903, while Hawaii came within touching distance of 400,000 tons that same year. Brazilian production shifted south from Bahia (the "old" cane growing region of the eighteenth and nineteenth century) toward Minas Gerais and São Paulo. Sugar output increased briskly from 100,000 tons in 1870 to 320,000 in 1900. By 1929, Brazil surpassed the 1 million ton marker. Louisiana was by no means an irrelevant player in the global cane sugar economy, but it simply could not keep up. The 1904 crop of 355,000 tons was the largest yet manufactured in the state and not matched again until the 1940s. Hawaiian sugar growers, by contrast, outstretched Louisiana's crop by 1903 and continued to increase production. On the eve of the Japanese attack on Pearl Harbor, sugar production on the Hawaiian Islands surpassed 1 million tons. Other major cane producers, South Africa, Peru, and Mexico, sharply increased production in the 1920s, but Cuba remained the undisputed monarch of global sugar. In 1925, Cuban planters manufactured more than 5 million tons, much of it bound for the United States.[28]

Louisiana producers simply could not compete in the global sugar race. New threats, however, abounded. In particular, sugar beets represented a fresh challenge on the global and domestic stage. During the second half of the nineteenth century, beet sugar production increased globally from 160,000 tons in 1850 to 6.8 million tons in 1900. Refined sugar beets produce a sugar almost indistinguishable from that of tropical cane and are readily cultivated in northern Europe and North America. By midcentury sugar beet production surged, particularly in France and Germany, and by the early 1880s beet sugar production outstripped international cane supplies. Belgium alone equaled the output of the British West Indies, while Germany produced more sugar than the Caribbean islands combined. During the 1890s, beets accounted for almost 60 percent of world sugar production. With European beet production in wartime doldrums from 1914 to 1918, cane growers rallied, though beets recovered in the interwar years, and, as Europe descended into the Second World War, beet sugar surpassed 11 million tons in 1939. The United States played second fiddle to European beet manufacturers from the late nineteenth to mid-twentieth centuries. Germany and Russia led the European producers, but beets were grown from Sweden to Spain and from Belgium to the Baltic. American beet farmers produced relatively insignificant amounts of sugar in the 1870s and 1880s (between 500 and 2,000 tons), though, in the first decade of the twentieth century, production increased. In 1911, US beet sugar amounted to 500,000 tons; by 1920, that figure had more than doubled, and, in 1939, farmers in the midwestern states produced almost 2 million tons of beet sugar. To stem this domestic and international challenge, Louisiana sugar planters lobbied hard for domestic protection, securing safeguards through bounties via the McKinley Tariff of 1890 and the Dingley Tariff of 1897, the latter being protectionist duties that remained largely in effect until 1914.[29]

American cane farmers faced a perfect storm by the eve of World War I. Four of the largest cane sugar economies—Hawaii, Puerto Rico, Cuba, and the Philippines—sold their produce duty free (or at the substantially reduced rates following the 1903 and 1909 reciprocity treaties), and the US beet industry increasingly swamped domestic markets with refined sugars. Domestic cane sugar manufacturers faced additional difficulties, for, while imported sugar often arrived refined and market ready, most Louisiana sugar sold raw or clarified and required refining into high-grade white granulated sugar. Louisiana producers accordingly sold into the worst, most undifferentiated market possible; they had reached commodity hell. Big business did nothing to ease the tightened straits that Louisiana producers encountered. The American Sugar Refining Company, established 1888 with its headquarters in Brooklyn, swiftly developed an iron grip over the US market, suppressing raw sugar prices by aggressively purchasing and by supporting legislation that allowed raw sugars to enter the nation practically duty free.[30]

Fall of the Plantation Order

Global competition and US imperial expansion presented major obstacles to the maintenance of domestic US cane sugar monoculture. In their struggle to remain competitive, however, American cane producers undertook a major reorganization of the sugar industry. The traditional structure based on the highly individualized plantation system, where landowners grew cane and then processed it in their own mills, gave way to the separation of growing and processing stages. This was a global phenomenon, for the cost and complexity of sugar processing machinery sharply increased, ensuring that most growers could no longer afford their own technologically advanced, commercially competitive mills. Centralized milling thus emerged during the 1880s, with sugar processing focused at just a few capital-intensive mills. This process of business consolidation brought the plantation system to its close. American cane growers were by no means distinct in encountering the end of the highly individualized plantation order of New World sugar. In Cuba, a complete revolution in productive structures also began in the 1880s, and, as historian Laird Bergad observes, these changes were the "coup de grace to the old planter class." Unable to master either land, capital, or labor following slave emancipation, sugar lords throughout the tropics underwent their own process of differentiation. Successful mill owners modernized and became planter-industrialists, whereas owners of outdated mills who lacked adequate capital to modernize became cane farmers. The vast majority of landlords and former slaveholders remained in this second category. No longer capable of owning a vertically integrated operation that combined the agricultural and processing stages, landlords encountered an industry where sugar production was concentrated in just a few, often corporate, hands. Foreign capital (mostly US) further supplanted the erstwhile dominion of the local planter elite, who faced a changing order on the land. Throughout the Americas, surviving mills were technologically modernized, the division of the sugar industry into agricultural and industrial components

began in earnest, and centralized milling advanced, all at the expense
of the traditional plantation.[31]

In many cane sugar societies, the land-extensive, labor-intensive
plantation gave way to tenancy, sharecropping, and smallholding arrangements. Gang labor certainly continued, particularly during harvest, but, with the arbitrary discipline of enslaved labor finally brought
to a close, the massed labor crews of earlier eras disintegrated in favor
of smaller work gangs, often staffed by a mix of white, black, and foreign workers. In Cuba and Puerto Rico, former slaves and cane workers overwhelmingly toiled on subdivided plantations, renting *colonias*
and raising cane for industrialized central factories (*centrales*). Indeed,
in these two societies central milling emerged not just out of economic necessity but as a product and reaction to abolition. Even the
terminology associated with the plantation complex changed. *Centrales* replaced the old plantation *ingenios* (small nineteenth-century
sugar mills) in Cuba and Puerto Rico, central *usinas* (factories) super-
seded Brazilian *enghenos*, while in Louisiana central factories replaced
the once dominant plantations at the pinnacle of the production system. Mill owners set production targets and prices, they laid railroad
track to expedite cane supplies from the mill's hinterland, and, in
some cases, they acquired and amalgamated landholdings. In all cane
economies, central mills ramped up production, consolidating their
dominance over the industry. These processes advanced haltingly in
some locations, rapidly in others. By 1900, however, New World sugar
production showed strong oligopolistic tendencies, which were enhanced still further by the monopolistic dominance of the sugar refining industry, particularly in the United States. Under these cir-
cumstances, the social organization of production associated with
the plantation system fractured, and with it the class prerogatives of
the landed class began to erode. In its place, the central factory
emerged as the new institutional framework. Owned by members of
a new planter class, combining Northern investors, some survivors
of the prewar elite, and New Orleans businesspeople, the sugar cen-
trals were remote in spirit and practice from the independence and

autonomy of the stand-alone plantation. Stripped of a direct stake in the means of production, former grandees now found themselves to be dependent clients of mill owners and refinery bosses in distant Northern cities.[32]

Louisiana's march toward centralized production also began in the 1880s but not exactly for the same reasons as in Cuba and Brazil. There, the abolition of slavery (1886 and 1888) prompted a labor crisis. With former slaves unwilling to toil as they had under bondage, landlords subdivided their estates into small rental plots. This process ended the dominance of the traditional sugar production complex and paved the route to centralized milling. In Louisiana, by contrast, state and planter forces colluded with the LSPA to resolve (albeit imperfectly) the labor problem by the late 1880s. Louisiana planters nevertheless faced a hostile and challenging economic climate. Although planters could not stem the tide of cheap sugars from Hawaii and the Caribbean, as they swiftly learned, mechanization offered domestic cane farmers a competitive advantage and a means maintain a share, although a decreasing one, of the US sugar market.

Modernization, however, proved expensive. For more than a decade after the Civil War, planters lacked the capital and business confidence to modernize their sugar facilities. By the early 1880s, however, the LSPA urged sugar manufacturers to embrace science and new technology. Greater manufacturing efficiency, they charged, would enable them to remain competitive. Some cane farmers borrowed from the beet sugar industry and tested diffusion techniques, which extracted sucrose by repeatedly immersing cane in water. The majority, however, embraced the vacuum technology that inventors like Rillieux pioneered in the 1840s. Indeed, low-pressure vacuum pans and mechanized milling proved to be the industry standard by 1900. Larger and more powerful rollers increased the juice-extraction process while centrifugal machines employing high-speed spinning drums to separate sugar and syrup further improved the extraction of higher-grade sugar. Professional chemists worked alongside sugar makers, testing the alkalinity and acidity of the cane juice and perfecting the use of optical polariscopes to determine sugar strength. Operating costs soared as new machinery and staff entered the sugarhouse. In 1860, sugar plantations ordinarily included $12,000 of machinery. By 1907, this figure had increased to $170,000. Many planters could not afford the step change in expenditure, and although some combined in partnership agreements, the total number of mills fell swiftly. In 1879, 1,111 mills operated; twenty years later, 275 ground cane; by 1929, just 70 sugar factories operated in Louisiana. Landlords who had previously operated stand-alone mills—like their counterparts in other tropical societies—found it more advantageous to sell their cane to local factories than to modernize.[33]

Those who remained, however, benefited from higher yields, improved sugar recovery rates, better sugars, and economies of scale. By 1914, the average sugar factory ground 25,000 tons of cane, from 1,700 acres, much of which was linked to the factory by a network of railroads. Successful planters like Mary Ann Patout often took several years to weather the transition from plantation to central factory. In 1887, Patout began that process, securing contracts with neighboring farmers for their cane, replacing her three-roller mill with a more powerful six-roller model, laying tracks across her estate, and acquiring multiple-effect evaporators before making the final transition to central factory in the mid-1890s. Although the two-cents-per-pound bounty on domestic vacuum sugar under the McKinley Tariff provided a welcome incentive for expansion, planters like Patout carefully and guardedly modernized, limiting their exposure to risk. She was right to do so. Despite boosting production to almost 1,500 tons per factory, the lower cane yields in subtropical Louisiana continued to emasculate regional competitiveness.[34]

The LSPA additionally sought to modernize American cane sugar through the application of science. Working with the US Department of Agriculture and funded with Northern capital, the LSPA established research plantations where new machinery could undergo trials and new cane breeds could be cultivated. In 1885, they established the sugar experiment station in Audubon Park, New Orleans, on the property where Boré first granulated sugar, before finally relocating to Louisiana State University in 1897, where the sugar institute remains.

Under the direction of William C. Stubbs, researchers at the Audubon station conducted agricultural, chemical, and engineering experiments. As Stubbs observed before the House of Representatives Ways and Means Committee, "there is a scientific as well as a politico-economic side" to the domestic sugar industry. The successful planter "requires a comprehensive knowledge of agriculture, mathematics, mechanics, mechanical engineering, drawing and sugar making." Stubbs was alone in neither his conclusions nor the professionalization of sugar training. Across the cane world, horticulturists, biochemists, and engineers gathered in sugar experiment stations, the most important of which were located in Java, Barbados, and Hawaii. Like much of the cane industry, sugar research was modernized and institutionalized by 1900. The sugar stations and their allied universities advanced biotechnology in a globalized industry where US cane agronomy and American science still played a significant international role.[35]

The same could not be said for Louisiana sugar. The disastrous crop of 1912, the spread of mosaic disease (and a devastating decline in sugar outputs), and the further withdrawal of field labor undermined an already enfeebled industry. The number of mills declined as the process of consolidation advanced apace. Cash-strapped landlords subdivided their estates into tenant-operated farms, finally recognizing that tenants then could grow cane more cheaply than could gang labor. The Underwood Tariff reduced sugar duties still further, and in 1916 free sugar became law. It was, the *Louisiana Planter* abhorred, "one of the most violent intrusions of the general government that has ever occurred in this country." American cane sugar rallied in two new geographic areas, Texas and Florida. Texan production increased sharply in the first decades of the twentieth century, and by 1907 eight sugar factories operated in the state. At Sugar Land, near Houston, E. H. Cunnington combined his own cane with Cuban sugar imports to establish a major regional refinery. The temporary rise in the value of cane during World War I likewise prompted investors to purchase large tracts of cane land in the Florida Everglades. Sugar outputs, nevertheless, remained small until the 1930s, when the United States

Sugar Corporation expanded operations and practically monopolized sugar development in southern Florida until the 1950s.[36]

Sugar cane is still grown in Louisiana, and it remains a thriving regional business. Like its tropical neighbors to the south, the story of nineteenth-century American sugar nevertheless mirrored the rise and fall of the plantation complex. In Jamaica, Barbados, and Brazil, this process took several centuries—and it remains as yet an unfinished process in many parts of the tropics—in the United States, sugar reigned only briefly. The wealth of the antebellum sugar elite, however, derived from the same sources that underpinned the enrichment of plantocrats elsewhere. American cane producers tapped into a vast consumer-led boom for sucrose, and they enjoyed, albeit sporadically, tariff protection from the US government. Under these beneficial trade conditions, and with a large pool of enslaved labor toiling in a brutal violent regime, US sugar expanded, and by the mid-nineteenth century American slaveholders in the lower Mississippi valley oversaw a relatively competitive and large sugar industry. The difficulties faced by American land and labor lords, however, were not widely different from those of plantation owners in the tropics or elsewhere in the South. Emancipation radically transformed labor relations, and although regional sugar planters attempted to assert their authority in the decades after the Civil War, Louisiana's cane fields were the scene of wild-cat strikes and sustained worker-employer conflict until the mid-1880s. Planters attempted to resolve the so-called labor problem with Chinese and European workers, but their efforts failed. By 1885, planters once again relied on African American crews to conduct hard, grim labor.

In the aftermath of the Civil War and facing increased competition from domestic beet sugar and global cane competition, US sugar producers struggled to remain competitive. The new vacuum and centrifugal technology proved prohibitively costly, and, like their counterparts in Cuba, Puerto Rico, and elsewhere, American planters ceded control of the industry to central factories. Free trade and US imperialism hit Louisiana's sugar interests hard. Duty-free Hawaiian sugar and reduced tariffs on Cuban sugar decimated an already weakened industry. By 1920, America's domestic cane sugar industry was on a lifeline—only a degree of sustained tariff protection kept Louisiana's sugar industry operational.

The plantation system upon which the success of New World rested for three centuries ultimately collapsed in the final years of the nineteenth century. For much of that century, however, sugar remained a fundamental determinant in the economic and social relations of production. It defined the plantation system and uniquely shaped enslaved and postemancipation labor systems across the Americas, Louisiana included. Like their compatriots in the nineteenth-century rice or twentieth-century tobacco industries, domestic cane farmers faced commodity hell. Unable to compete in an international market, US cane producers nevertheless held fast to the tariff as the sole means to guarantee profits. Free trade, however, blasted cold comfort through the screen doors of Louisiana's crumbling plantation homes. Buffeted by trade winds that blew from the Pacific, the Indian Ocean, the Caribbean, and the beet fields of the American Midwest, the historic heart of America's cane sugar industry began its long decline.

BARBARA HAHN

Tobacco's Commodity Route

❧

THERE IS A MYSTERY about tobacco that can be answered only historically: What are the varietal types, and how did they develop? In the
American colonies, around the Chesapeake Bay, most of the British
settlers grew what Lewis Cecil Gray (the dean of Southern antebellum agricultural history) called the "two great colonial types," Orinoco and Sweet Scented. Today, the US Department of Agriculture
(USDA), founded during the Civil War, has identified finer distinctions. The USDA formally named the tobacco types in 1925, and each
is defined along three axes: where it is from, what it is for, and what
has been done to produce it. Examples include Connecticut Shade-
Grown Cuban-Seed Cigar Leaf, Eastern Dark Fire-Cured Tobacco of
Kentucky and Tennessee, Western Dark Fire-Cured Tobacco of Kentucky and Tennessee, and Bright Flue-Cured Cigarette Tobacco of
North Carolina and Southside Virginia. How were these types distinguished from one another? Specific institutions, including both
government regulations and trade relationships, created incentive
structures for unique cultivation methods in particular regions that
produced leaf with characteristics that served specific markets. This
historical process constructed and codified the varietal types. Plant
types usually assumed to be naturally distinct were in fact products
made by human choice, market needs, and the regulatory culture of
the tobacco industry.[1]

Unlike the commodity hell into which the other crops in this book ultimately descended—in which price competition among undifferentiated goods plunged planters into perdition—tobacco's commodification is a more complex story. At first, tobacco planters in the American South benefited, as did rice and sugar producers, from the mercantilist laws of the empire. After independence, however, its postharvest processing grew into a fully realized industry that manufactured tobacco-based consumer goods for global markets. At the same time, merchants found new markets, and growers specialized production methods to meet them. Once that task was complete—once each tobacco type described an interchangeable commodity—the process familiar from the chapters on rice and sugar could begin in earnest. As this chapter demonstrates, tobacco's eventual descent into commodity hell resulted in violent resistance in the twentieth century. A few decades later, the renewal of government protections against price-cutting competition defined tobacco types that paradoxically supported commodification. Tobacco varieties do economic work, in other words. While the causes of varietal differentiation are historical and therefore complex, their effects are clear and parsimonious (the principle that the fewest possible assumptions should be made when formulating an explanation), as economists prefer.

Tobacco types developed historically—rather than biologically— because there is in fact very little genetic difference among them. These lessons were not immediately appreciated. By 1936, however, government geneticists had determined that bright and dark tobaccos from Virginia were "so similar as to be almost indistinguishable," although their visible, sensible, morphological characteristics were distinct. They recognized that when the cultivation of bright cigarette tobacco had begun to replace dark colonial tobacco after the Civil War, "[t]here was no significant change in the varieties of seed used," and "the present strains of the Orinoco as a whole do not differ greatly from those employed originally." Late nineteenth-century tobacco types were thus fundamentally similar to the tobacco exported from colonial Jamestown, and by 2007—four centuries after John Rolfe famously followed local Powhatan chiefs in planting Virginia tobacco in the 1610s—a paper investigating methods of genetic testing described "the low level of genetic diversity within and among cultivated tobacco types."[2]

Some plant species have varietal types that occur in the seeds, of course, which produce very different commodities—wine and grapes are an excellent example. Even then, however, care must be taken to prevent mutations and evolution: modern seed breeders prefer the term *cultivar* to *varietal*, since each type is a product of ongoing human choice and intervention. Historical actors, too—the people who grew tobacco or bought it or marketed or manufactured it—did not regularly assume that the different varieties of the leaf came from the seed. Instead, they recognized that different planting and curing methods produced distinct tastes and marketable qualities. In 1846, a planter wrote his merchant the request to "[t]ell what colour you want tobacco next year," while another merchant wrote a different farmer in 1872 that his crop had "plenty of size for shipping, but all too much of a Manufacturing flavor for that purpose." This letter described shipping and manufacturing tobaccos as particular types with unique characteristics that both buyer and grower understood and would recognize. As late as 1879, similar correspondence contained the advice that "[w]e hope you sun cured and flue cured your crop this year. You cant make any other sort of tobacco that will buy you." In none of these cases did the writer think that the characteristics in the finished commodity had much relationship to its seeds. Technological choices did not rely on natural categories.[3]

Genetics cannot entirely account for the different tobacco types, and historical actors did not recognize their existence until relatively recently. When things seem natural but are not, the history of technology provides methods for understanding how and when they were constructed. As other chapters have shown, changing cultivation technologies had the power to shift economic fundamentals, as irrigating rice and processing sugar both changed the scale on which those staples were produced in the American South. Likewise, changing economic factors can demand new technologies, as emancipation changed the capital requirements of rice, cotton, sugar, and tobacco production and, with them, their cultivation systems. Different periods of American history had different laws and valued economic factors in different ways, and as a result they also had different production systems for tobacco. Thus, tobacco types defined by technologies of production emerged at different times." Regulations in colonial Chesapeake shaped agricultural methods and mediated the market relations between growers and their markets. Then, independence changed cultivation systems to meet wider markets with an array of preferences, while westward expansion of the crop into new locations— Kentucky in particular—created new tobacco types in new regions. Later, the Civil War and emancipation transformed elements of the production system, especially the harvest and curing methods that today help define regional tobacco types and their specific markets— they are often defined as fire cured or flue cured, for example. New postbellum processes fitted neatly into late nineteenth-century marketing systems among merchants, storekeepers, landlords, tenants, and sharecroppers who sold the crop and paid their annual bills. With the New Deal and the federal government's limits on production (in exchange for guaranteeing the prices farmers received for their goods), the USDA told twentieth-century farmers not only how much they could grow but of what kind of leaf. This locked into place the production system that had emerged from the Civil War. The New Deal therefore made possible the modern classification of the "generic" leaf into "specific" types.[4]

Each preceding chapter focused, to a greater or lesser extent, on the creation of domestic and international markets for the South's principal plantation staples. This chapter turns a new corner: whereas American rice and sugar suffered—while US cotton triumphed—in undifferentiated markets, the focus in this final case study is on tobacco's domestic and international markets and the history of the trade routes through which tobacco leaf met specific demands. Well-established commercial relationships (dating back to the colonial era) had helped people to judge the value of leaf and ascertain its desirable characteristics in transactions, while buyers could count on these by knowing that it came from seasoned producers. Meanwhile, the institutions that mediated these economic relationships—the political economies of particular periods—added cultural and regulatory contexts for the cultivation systems and changing technologies to produce tobacco. Across time, geography, and local context, tobacco types that were developed in particular regions, featuring traits desired in particular markets, were ultimately produced by specific techniques that reliably delivered those desirable characteristics. In turn, those techniques altered when the political economy underwent one change after another. That is how today's tobacco types came into existence and came to seem natural.

Colonial Regulation

The English were latecomers to the race for New World territory. They found no gold to compete with the Spanish conquistadors, and only a little of the territory they claimed as their own would produce sugar, the first crop of European imperial expansion. English settlers did eventually find a crop to grow in place of their hopes of easy riches. They found tobacco, and, according to some accounts, the first shipload of leaf brought such prices that the colonists at Jamestown planted tobacco in the streets. It took time for the metropolitan masters to find a range of markets, but, when the colonizers of the Chesapeake Bay and its tributary rivers sent their first "rolls" of tobacco to the Crown as an experiment in the 1610s, they were extraordinarily lucky: the plant they produced was addictive. Still, when prices fell, new customers and more efficient production technologies often rapidly took up the slack.[5]

Even short periods of lower prices, however, were difficult for settlers to endure. Five years after the first export, the 1617 boom went bust. In response to that jarring downturn in tobacco's value, the burgesses (colonial Virginia's lawmakers) tried to raise the price of the colony's crop. They undertook to regulate the market in hopes of boosting the value of their settlers' produce. Their first efforts attempted to control the quantity grown by Virginia's planters, relying on a simple supply-and-demand relationship: produce less tobacco, and what is grown will bring a higher price. Known as the "stint laws," these regulations tried to limit growers to a certain number of plants per "headd." For example, "two hundred pound for a Master of a family and one hundred and a quarter for every servant." Another effort allowed three thousand plants per tithable person "workeing the ground" or "where the familie consisteth of children and woemen which doe not worke in the ground . . . not above 1000 plants." Every attempt to assign quantity sown or sold per person raised the question of who was a legal person—as women, children, servants, and slaves were not. Stint laws also appeared to favor growers with more resources, as more hands in the fields meant more plants allowed. The burgesses went on experimenting with the political economy.[6]

In 1713, and then again in 1730, laws passed by the House of Burgesses took a different tack. Instead of directly controlling quantity, the new laws instead attempted to raise the quality of leaf produced in the colony. They forbade the sale of second-growth tobacco of any kind. Suckers, a kind of second leaf that grows from the juncture where leaf meets stalk, could not legally be sold. Neither could ratoons, the leaves that grow from the stump once the plant has been cut down as harvest. Only first-growth leaves from the first harvest of the plant were marketable, and an elaborate government inspection system ensured it. Tobacco determined by the inspectors to be trashy would be burned. Small planters protested, but violent opposition eventually gave way—the burning of tobacco warehouses, a favored form of protest in tobacco country, became "punishable by death." Concessions helped assuage pent-up hostility: while the eighteenth-century inspection laws may have required the burning of trashy tobacco, they did allow more warehouses and the distribution of negotiable receipts for the hogsheads (large wooden barrels containing approximately a thousand pounds of tobacco) that had passed inspection. These tobacco notes supplied a medium of exchange—tobacco became money and paid colonial salaries—which additionally eased commerce. Finally, a price rise in the mid-1730s softened opposition.[7]

The inspection laws had two effects crucial for the eventual emergence of tobacco's varietal types. First, they provided incentives for a cultivation system—a technological system of agricultural production—that over the next fifty years solidified into what scholars have called the "Chesapeake system" of tobacco cultivation. The law prohibiting the sale of second growths and trash allowed only first-growth leaves to reach the market. Growers therefore had incentives to make those leaves as big and heavy and good as they could. They left the leaves growing on the stalk as long as possible, then harvested them all at once, as fast as possible before the frost. Harvest consisted of chopping the plant down and splitting the stalk (almost all the way down) and flipping it over, hanging the split stem over a stick for curing. As with sugar, harvest initiated a rapid, labor-intensive series of processes to cure or stabilize the leaves, to prevent their rotting. Some planters performed various acts of sweating or wilting before bringing the leaf into the barn for curing, but it is not clear that their methods created specific predictable results in the leaves. Choosing how to cure tobacco meant paying attention to the weather—a rainy season might demand some small fires in the barn, while dry weather could allow curing the leaf with air alone. Once curing was complete, plucking the leaves off the stalk and preparing them for market could wait, and usually did wait for some months, until spring rains made the leaf more manipulable. Marketing the leaf usually waited until the next year; in other words, the entire cultivation cycle could last eighteen months or longer.[8]

Neighbors or strangers might offer to buy tobacco before it was prepared for inspection and export sales, however. They might do the work required for selling and wait for the eventual sale to claim more of the agricultural product's ultimate value. Or they might not—the possibility of selling early leads the historian to recognize the second unintended consequence of the inspection laws. The laws actually created two categories of tobacco: one intended for export and another only good enough to stay home. These quality differences fed into a distinction that would emerge between shipping and manufacturing tobaccos in the nineteenth century evidenced in a 1872 letter describing leaf that had "plenty of size for [export] shipping" but "a Manufacturing [cheaper, domestic] flavor." These two effects of the colonial regulatory environment continued to impact tobacco culture after independence, into the nineteenth century and beyond.[9]

Institutions—like laws and technology—accrue power and authority over time. They become benchmarks, industry standards, even norms. The colonial inspection laws demonstrate one way that can happen: from the seventeenth century on, the laws became expressed in the system of production—in effect, shaping the way things were done. Understood this way, technology does not determine human action—instead, human action shapes technology. "Closure," to use the language of science and technology studies, can turn a technology into a black box, an unexamined device for accomplishing a specific human purpose. And so it was with tobacco where the cultivation methods as well as the larger system of production that contained them (labor requirements, marketing methods) fitted together so tidily that they came to seem natural, as if they were the requirements of the plant or the demands of the markets. Moreover, they became constraints. The inspection laws were not the only influence on this naturalization of technology—an established method employs culture and social hierarchies as well as technology. Assumptions about the work of different kinds of people belonging to different social groups, men and women, servants and children, shaped production as surely as did the inspection or stint laws.[10] But laws are easier to assign a causative role than is culture, their influences are simpler to trace, and of course they also bear the marks of their cultural contexts. The inspection laws also demonstrate that in the early regulation of markets—from almost the dawn of traditional American history, laws have mediated and influenced markets in profound ways. Indeed, as the history of tobacco inspection laws makes clear, markets were never entirely free; they were regulated and conditioned by laws that reflected economic and market perspectives of the time.

Comparing Cultivation Methods

The impact of colonial and imperial institutions on the systems of tobacco production in the English Chesapeake appears most clearly when compared with the tobacco cultivation systems that developed at other times and places in a range of regulatory environments. Unlike rice and cotton and sugar, tobacco was an indigenous continental product well before the arrival of Europeans. The Native American tribes of the Great Plains had different rules than did the English settlers of Virginia and therefore had other methods of producing tobacco. For them, consumption was religious ritual. Many groups in this region preferred to smoke flowers rather than the leaves. For them, harvest began at midsummer, when the blossoms first appeared. Deadheading the blooms produced new ones, and Mandan, Hidatsa, and Arikara tribes thereby had a new harvest every four days. These Native American groups cultivated and harvested the flowers that the Virginia lawmakers had classified as worthless refuse.[11]

Even European settlers had different technologies depending on their national cultures. The French colonists of eighteenth-century Louisiana, for example, also began their harvest at midsummer. Like the English Virginians, however, they favored leaves over flowers. French Louisianans began their harvest when the suckers first appeared. They plucked the first leaves and allowed the second growths to mature as leaves, allowed the suckers to grow to full size, then harvested those, when new ones appeared. To them, the suckers were simply another set of leaves—not the trash that Virginia inspectors had to burn. Harvest lasted all through the summer in French Louisiana, which permitted several sets of suckers to mature and reach harvest. Without inspection laws, the marketing methods of French colonists reflected their long harvest of small quantities. They tied up leaf into what they called carottes and packed it in boxes, and the French government tobacco monopoly (the *regie*) promised to take all they offered. "It was said that several cuttings were obtainable in a single year," according to Lewis Cecil Gray. "The quality of the product was reported excellent, better than that of Virginia," although to Virginians who prized only the first growth, these suckers were not even leaves.[12]

Alternative methods to the Chesapeake system persisted in other locations. Descriptions of tobacco in Spanish colonies, for example, appeared to describe an entirely different plant than that of the Chesapeake because the regions' growers took advantage of different plant processes. The Spanish had been the first Europeans to adopt tobacco. Their methods, like those of the French, took advantage of the second growths that Virginia's burgesses had the inspectors burn. The Spanish, however, cultivated tobacco in ratoons, in ways not dissimilar to sugar cultivation where farmers also reaped a second (and sometimes third) return from the stubble of the previous crop. Ratoons grew after the whole tobacco plant was harvested and sprang from the remains left in the ground.[13] In 1800, one English author (in his explanation of the Chesapeake system to an audience that had recently lost its colonies), said that ratoons were "of a sufficient quality for smoking, and might become preferred in the weaker kinds of snuff." While ratoons were not ideal, English authorities rejected these plants not because of market and consumer demand but because colonial laws had established the way tobacco "should" be grown. In reality, of course, ratoons provided abundant evidence of what second-growth tobacco could become—they were good enough for smoking and even for some kinds of snuff.[14]

Because Virginia burgesses had forbidden the sale of second growths such as suckers and ratoons, the methods for producing them had disappeared in Virginia by the time of independence. The technology for cultivating tobacco in the region, the long-standing Chesapeake system of leaf production, instead allowed the sale of only first-growth leaves. This meant that the inspection laws created a "peak labor demand" at first-growth harvest, which in turn made slave labor central to the region's economy. Laws distinguishing slaves from other laborers had been on Virginia's books since the 1660s, and the existence of a bound labor force made possible the adoption of an abrupt, rapid, and laborious group of tasks related to harvest and curing. Once the Chesapeake system reached a point of stabilization (and was widely applied by tobacco cultivators), its tasks made larger workforces profitable and required their year-round employment.[15] If 1713 and 1730 accordingly mark the date of effective inspection laws, economic historians have pointed to a "steady upward drift" in the size of farms and in the proportion of them using slaves after 1720. What had been a crop suited to smallholders began to favor large-scale production—a preference that persisted even after it became economically irrational, with major tobacco-growing families falling into debt to maintain their big houses and plantings. Although historians have provided many different reasons to account for the so-called labor switch from free indentured servants to enslaved African labor in the Chesapeake, it is plainly clear that the tobacco planters' commitment to plantation production using slave labor can be traced to the harvest method and—in part—to the inspection laws that privileged the labor-intensive system of harvesting just first-growth leaves.[16]

Independence and New Markets

The Virginia legislators intended one result from these efforts at market regulation—higher prices from tobacco's buyers. In the colonial period, the buyers were British. Mercantilism assumed that colonial production existed to benefit the imperial metropolis. England's Navigation Acts, first passed in 1651 and amended regularly thereafter, prohibited the sale of settlers' produce to anyone but the English, in any but English ships. Should a Dutch ship appear at a plantation dock and its captain offer to buy any available hogsheads of tobacco, selling would have been illegal—though, over time, plenty of people probably did anyway. Nonetheless, imperial laws dictated that tobacco buyers filter their demands through England's merchant firms. In exchange for this restriction, the British refrained from growing tobacco anywhere other than the Chesapeake. Virginia tobacco ultimately found markets around the world as different regions picked up the nicotine habit. Yet, for much of the seventeenth and eighteenth centuries, Chesapeake-grown tobacco was available legally only through metropolitan sources, since Virginians had to sell their goods to British buyers before it reached other markets.[17]

The Navigation Acts gave the metropolitan merchants a brisk business in what was called "re-exporting," in which Chesapeake leaf entered British ports before being sold around the world. Sometimes it just sat in the ship; sometimes it entered a warehouse; sometimes someone added a little value before sending it on its way. Always, the crown skimmed off some revenue before exporting its colonial produce to a different market. Profits from re-exporting mattered to England. On the eve of the American Revolution, between 85 and 90 percent of the leaf shipped to England from the colonies was re-exported elsewhere. In this way, the Navigation Acts shaped trade relationships, in that British colonists saw world markets mostly through the descriptions and accounts of transactions sent by their English and Scottish merchants. British colonists accordingly had to interpret market demand through merchant instructions.[18]

Independence gave Americans the opportunity to meet those markets directly. New markets, though, required new preparations of the leaf to meet more varied demands. Widening markets usually call forth product differentiation, and agricultural commodities are no exception. The French were notoriously finicky and selective. Changing fashions among French buyers required adjusting the curing methods in an effort to make "fancy colored tobacco," ranging from piebald and calico to green streak, or fawn or straw or hickory-leaf color, as demand dictated.[19] One merchant described their preferences as follows: "[t]he varities of the kinds they take are so great that a sample would be of very little use to you in sellecting." Spaniards, by contrast, apparently liked tobacco "of very *fine*, *sweet*, *brown colour*" and, in 1835, expected to find suitable leaf in Richmond markets. In Holland and Germany, "[b]ecause they use tobacco principally for smoking . . . an inferior cheap article will do," and Virginia planters disposed of their worse leaf on those markets. Different markets shaped new technologies and systems of production that created unique commodities for each national palate. In this way, independence marked an important institutional shift in the eventual development of tobacco types.[20]

Of course, the English continued to buy American tobacco in huge quantities even after independence. The data are startling: between 1820 and 1840, Britain still imported 30 percent of all Virginia's export leaf, and, because they took more leaf of better quality, they actually received 46 percent of Virginia tobacco's export value. Which is to say that fifty years after George Washington's presidency, Britain took in nearly half the value of leaf exported from its former colony. They still re-exported nearly half of that, and, thus, even after independence they still mediated between American growers and merchants and the markets for their goods. While an argument can be made that the United States sought independence at least partly to meet its markets more directly, the long-standing institutions of Anglo-American trade (buildings, systems, ports, and practices) worked against that goal. The British merchants had so much practice in the trade and had built such convenient infrastructure and institutions that they still dominated the export market.[21]

It was accretion of institutions, in other words: the British Navigation Acts continued to act upon even the independent one-time colonies. So did the inspection laws those colonies had imposed on themselves. As the nineteenth century began, the second effect of the inspection laws began to emerge and influence the history of tobacco types. The development of a domestic tobacco-manufacturing industry blossomed from its roots in early business regulation. Indeed, it emerged partly because of institutions accumulating over time. Virginia's colonial burgesses had made efforts to raise the price their constituents' tobacco would bring in British markets. They had created, therefore, a distinction between leaf for export and leaf that stayed home. The laws thus provided a supply structure that stimulated domestic manufacturing.

Industrialization

The tobacco industry goes back a long way, but it first became an active part of the historical record in the nineteenth century. As early as the 1820s, accounts sales—which merchants used to explain the sales of farm produce—indicated distinct prices for tobacco "passed" and "refused" at inspection.[22] Moreover, distinctions between parcels for sale in Virginia often followed this line: one hogshead might be "good dry Shipping Tobacco's & very sweet," while another from the same crop was "of a Manufacturing quality." Everybody involved in the trade apparently knew the difference: "[S]hipping qualities and manfrs are in good demand," wrote Thomas Branch, a Richmond merchant.[23] Like Branch—who differentiated quality from behind a nineteenth-century trade ledger—distinguishing between "shipping" and "manufacturing" tobacco provides an important window into the development of tobacco types and their markets, each with its own demands or expectations.

If tobacco manufacturing provided another market use for tobacco, separate from the export markets, a question may arise: Where did the tobacco industry come from? None of the other staples discussed in this book witnessed domestic industrialization as tobacco did. According to one authority, after the Navigation Acts curtailed competition for Chesapeake goods, increases in freight costs led the colonists to manufacture their staple at home. Some sources described tobacco factories on the Rappahannock River (a Chesapeake tributary) by 1732; in 1750, Landon Carter, Virginia tobacco planter, introduced amendments to the colony's inspection laws—changes concerning the export of trash and allowing for the sale of second growths—laws specifically intended to protect domestic manufacturing. Henry Fitzhugh, another big name among colonial planters, likewise described tobacco that "sells better in the country" and often sold hogsheads at home. In the nearly two colonial centuries, it is safe to say that Americans consumed tobacco as well as producing it, and they found ways to make and distribute goods for the purpose. In addition, the Virginia legislature changed the inspection laws in the first generation after independence, providing new domestic markets for the leaf. In 1805, for instance, Virginia inspectors no longer had to burn the leaf they refused to export. Instead. they recognized that this tobacco had a market at home, even if it could not be sent overseas.[24]

The American tobacco industry produced brand-name consumer goods and sold them in both domestic and world markets as early as the 1830s. Long before Marlboro and Lucky Strike became household names, US producers were beginning to gain fame. Brands might be simply the names of their makers, such as Jno. M. Sutherlin, but more descriptive names included Crumpton & Paynes' Gold Leaf, Cherry Red, Luscious Luxury, and Wedding Cake. These brands described plug tobacco and lumps and twists, distinctively flavored and packaged for retail display and sale. The origins of that global behemoth, the US tobacco industry, have not often been explored. One reason is that the industrialization of the slave South does not fit tidily into the national narrative that attempts to explain the coming of the Civil War. Indeed, the textile industrialization of the North, with factories, machines, and production methods imported from England, usually contrasts with the increasing commitment of the South to agricultural production of cotton on plantations using slave labor. As the nation expanded into what became the West, tensions over these two systems and the cultures that accompanied them finally broke the nation in two. If cotton is the history of the US South in the nineteenth century, a claim that Sven Beckert uses to introduce his chapter, then tobacco provides an important counterexample—the industrialization of the slave South.[25]

New Growths in the Nineteenth Century

At the same time tobacco industrialized, westward expansion was pushing tobacco cultivation farther inland. This movement had begun during colonial times but accelerated with independence and the rapid admission of new states. The Northwest Territory carved out new states, beginning with Ohio in 1803 while, across the Ohio River, Kentucky had become the fifteenth state of the Union in 1792. In Kentucky, in particular, tobacco cultivation found a comfortable home. At first, the territory in Kentucky was an outgrowth of Virginia.[26] For tobacco to take hold on the frontier, however, its growers had to find markets. Their inland location provided access to the Gulf Coast trade with tobacco farmers shipping their goods into the Ohio and Mississippi River system, eventually all the way to New Orleans and the Gulf of Mexico. The Mississippi—moreover—was the border between the young nation and the empire of Spain, which wanted to buy American tobacco. Even after independence, the Louisiana Purchase of 1803, and admission to the Union, Kentucky leaf still mostly floated downstream to New Orleans.[27]

The Western leaf (as Kentucky tobacco was known) entered mostly export markets. Although tobacco manufacturing for local barter was well known in the backcountry—part of the self-sufficiency of frontier communities—Kentucky tobacco had a "spongy property," and, according to a government investigator in 1842, when "manufactured into 'lumps,' it loses its blackish rich color, and becomes, soon after exposure to the action of the atmosphere . . . what is termed 'frosted.'" Since locally made lumps did not survive distribution, most Western leaf served shipping rather than manufacturing purposes. Some Kentucky tobacco did enter the factories: in 1840, when Kentucky first made its appearance in the census data on manufacturing, it produced 7 percent of the value of the entire domestic tobacco manufacturing industry—a figure that rose to 8.8 percent in 1850 and 10 percent in 1860. Ten percent of the industry but bad frosted lumps: How to account for this contradiction?[28]

The Kentucky tobacco industry mostly engaged in semimanufacturing. Rather than making brand-name goods to be sold through to retailers and eventual consumers, Kentucky manufacturers usually performed a lucrative operation called "stemming." They removed the stems or midribs from leaves and repackaged the strips, as they were called, for sale through England to world markets. British tariffs imposed after independence provided incentives for this process. The strips were valuable enough to bear the added cost of the tariff, but the stems were not. Most of them would be removed during the manufacturing process and either discarded or made into goods of lesser value, so why pay tariff on their weight? Instead, the leaf was stemmed in Kentucky, and the strips sold to British brokers and manufacturers. Smugglers brought stems to England without paying the tariff, which created a black market. As a result, stemming the leaf intended for British markets became profitable US business, especially in Kentucky. The census called it manufacturing, but the strips were mostly exported.[29]

In the 1840s, Kentucky strips began to find a new market, as English merchants began to place the product in West Africa. Evans and Trokes of Liverpool wrote in 1840 to Towles & Soaper (a firm in western Kentucky), saying, "A recent demand for Africa has enabled holders to dispose of suitable qualities of leaf," and, two years later, "The imported has been nearly all from New Orleans and the principal Exports to Africa." Again, in 1843, "Of [the tobacco] Exported last month nearly the whole, or 219 [hogsheads] Kentucky leaf, principally brought here from London, were for Africa." By this time, the demand was such that merchants gave very specific instructions to another of their Kentucky correspondents for "preparing tobacco for Africa." They wanted a "dark colour, with an appearance of richness, not prizy or Sticky, Supple in Condition to keep Sweet & Sound & free from mould."[30] Brokered by English merchants, the preparation of Kentucky tobacco was—nonetheless—shaped by demands made in Africa. From London, Cape Town, and Louisville, the regular correspondence among merchants cemented trade relationships that linked supply from particular locations to demand around the world. For their part, African institutions provided incentives for leaf qualities with merchants at both ends of a transatlantic and transcontinental trade attempting to mediate the supply and demand for tobacco with specific color and characteristics. Wherever it was from and whatever it was for, these trade categories helped divide tobacco into recognizable types.

The Civil War

The Civil War and its aftermath transformed both tobacco agriculture and the tobacco industry, just as it did the other Southern staples. The changes it brought included not only new federal power and a new system of regulating the relationship between supply and demand but also a shift in costs and economic factors—for example, emancipation meant that human capital investment now became labor costs, while in the realm of regulation, agricultural science in the new USDA advised farmers how best to meet their markets. Production on war-torn landscapes also moved on to fresh fields. The center of tobacco agriculture accordingly shifted from Virginia to Kentucky, and the war-ravaged Old Dominion never regained its onetime dominance of cultivation. Virginians grew one-third the pounds of tobacco in 1870 that they had in 1860, while Kentucky tobacco production held steady. Likewise, in the manufacturing sector, Virginia had steadily produced until 1860 about 40 percent of the value of tobacco manufactured in the United States; this figure dropped below 10 percent in 1870 and stayed below 15 percent for the remainder of the century. The impact of war was to move tobacco to new locations as Virginia firms lost market share of both agricultural and industrial production.[31]

Policies and bureaucracies enacted by the federal government during the rebellion continued to be in force after the war, and they changed the institutions of both tobacco agriculture and the domestic tobacco industry. The new regulatory framework changed market relationships, that is to say, the mediation and negotiation between supply and demand. Taxation, emancipation, and the formation of the USDA in 1862 transformed incentives and the costs of production. Just as the cultivation and marketing methods of the Chesapeake had developed in response to the inspection laws, so the postbellum world wrought changes in tobacco technology too. As business incentives shifted, production technologies altered, with older patterns—focusing on slavery's peak labor demands and public inspection warehouses—replaced by new harvest, curing, and marketing methods.[32]

The tobacco industry changed, too, into its more familiar, turn-of-the-century, Big Business form. Taxing only manufactured tobacco contributed to the transformation of the antebellum tobacco industry and its consolidation into the monopolistic combination or trust of the Gilded Age. While scholars have generally ascribed the rise of the American Tobacco Company trust to the Bonsack cigarette-rolling machine, historians of technology more often seek to understand why a machine works—how it fits within a particular technological system, as well as its larger context—the sociotechnical web, as some have called it. This prevents technological determinism. Machines do not drop from the sky to have an effect, though scholars (following Alfred Chandler) have long accepted the argument that mechanizing cigarette production caused structural change in the tobacco industry.

History is more complicated than that. Structural changes and tax policy together inspired the increased production of cigarettes before the Bonsack machine made it easy, while changing consumer preferences from chewing to smoking tobacco waited much longer—really until World War I. The long gap between the American Tobacco Company's increased production and the transition to cigarette consumption indicates that the causes of change in the industry lie elsewhere than in the machine that saturated the market by increasing production.[33]

The assumption that varietals were natural, however, was expressed as a myth—or rather, as each tobacco type had its own supply-and-demand relationship as well as its own methods for creating the characteristics desired by consumers, each also had its own myth of origin. The origin myths of tobacco varietals tended to convey that a type's characteristics came from its seeds and that certain type-specific technologies best expressed those traits. While planters, growers, and traders did not share this belief, as mentioned above, myth-making is a phenomenon familiar to historians of technology. In fact, most technologies have myths of origin in which the device appears to drop from the sky or is assembled from the genius of the inventor. Classic cases of technological myths include not only the Bonsack cigarette-rolling machine but also Eli Whitney's familiar cotton gin and Hargreaves's spinning jenny that mechanized the industrial production of cotton thread. Whitney—the myth runs—left Yale for Savannah in 1792 and promptly invented the gin, which revolutionized cotton farming in one fell swoop. That Africans and Asians had developed ginning technology centuries before Whitney devised his mechanical engine to separate lint from cotton seeds mattered not—in America at least, Whitney became the master mythological inventor upon whom, he claimed, "Dame Fortune" had smiled.[34] In the case of the cultivation, harvest, curing, and marketing methods of the various tobacco types, their origin myths appeared in the post-bellum South and reflected the changing political economy initiated by war and emancipation. The Lost Cause of Civil War history and the Plantation Illusion, in which whites dreamed of happy slaves and benevolent masters, are the most famous examples of New South mythmaking. The emergence of tobacco types is another, and it fits very well with those themes.[35]

The Burley Story and the Black Patch Wars

The institutional shifts of the Civil War era included the emergence and classification of new tobacco types. One of these was White Burley Tobacco from Kentucky. Its myth of origin traces it back to 1863, when a pair of tenant farmers in Brown County, Ohio, ran short of seeds and crossed the Ohio River to borrow some from a Kentucky grower. "Although the seedlings grew sturdy and fine-textured, the dirty yellow leaf prompted the tenants to destroy the plants, believing them unhealthy or dwarfed." However, the following year, a more deliberate borrowing from Kentucky to Ohio led to similar results, but this time the brave tenant moved some of the dwarves from the seedbed to the field. They grew well and appeared "healthy and thrifty," with cream-colored stalks. The "freak tobacco" caused a sensation in the neighborhood and, when cured, the leaf came out bright yellow and smoked "bitter" and dry. The new type won several prizes at the 1867 St. Louis Fair and secured an excellent price in the Cincinnati market. Eventually it became the favored tobacco produced in the region.[36]

The dryness of the new tobacco type was considered its defining (and desirable) characteristic; burley is still thought great for absorbing artificial flavorings in many consumer goods, including both chewing tobacco and cigarettes. But remember that, back in 1842, sources described tobacco from Kentucky in similar terms, although then the dryness and ability to take on moisture made for bad frosted lumps. The "spongy property" meant that when "manufactured into lumps, [it] loses its blackish rich color, and becomes . . . 'frosted.'" Although burley was notionally a brand-new tobacco type, it possessed exactly the qualities that had distinguished tobacco from that region about 120 years earlier. It still served familiar markets, too: it entered the domestic manufacturing market and very often was stemmed into strips before selling. Because of increased prices for the newly desirable new type of leaf, however, little of the semimanufactured leaf sold to the English market. The price had become too high.[37]

In western Kentucky, old trade relationships maintained demand for other familiar products that also wore new names. The leaf once grown under such specific instructions from English merchants, tobacco prepared specifically for the African market, a crop whose characteristics included a "dark colour, with an appearance of richness," was now called Dark Fire-Cured Tobacco but still served very specific postbellum markets.[38] In the early twentieth century, after the rise of the American Tobacco Company, the regions that produced this tobacco type became the sites of the most violent agrarian radicalism in American history. The Black Patch Wars, as they were called, began in 1904, when farmers seeking higher prices began pooling their crops for cooperative marketing. They formed organizations and pledged to act as one, to withhold the crop from the market long enough to drive up the price. Not everybody joined in, however. Some farmers kept their crops outside the cooperative and then benefited when the shortage drove the buyers to offer higher prices for all available leaf.

Conflicts over pooling revealed deep-seated divisions in rural society, which escalated into violence in 1905, when night riders—masked men on horseback—blew up tobacco barns and warehouses in small Kentucky towns and harassed the merchants who represented distant leaf buyers. Things only got worse from there. In December 1906, 250 night riders seized the town of Princeton, Kentucky. Armed and wearing hoods, they rode into town, cut telephone and telegraph contact with the outside world, overwhelmed the police force and the fire department, dynamited one tobacco warehouse, and set fire to another. Half a million pounds of raw tobacco leaf burned furiously as citizens cowered in their homes. Although tobacco fetched higher prices the next year, the frenzy continued. Night riders burned Hopkinsville, Kentucky, in 1907. They did not shrink from beating and sometimes murdering resistors, witnesses, and sometimes just vulnerable black laborers peripheral to the conflict.[39]

Race—as ever in the history of the American South—was an important distinction among the region's tobacco growers. Robert Penn

Warren—poet, novelist, Southern agrarian, and Pulitzer Prize winner—was born in western Kentucky. In his novel of the Black Patch Wars, *Night Rider*, the hero received threats warning him to evict black tenants in favor of white families. When he failed to comply, his house was burned down. In real life, in March 1908, homegrown terrorists chased the entire African American population from Birmingham, in western Kentucky. A Louisville newspaper reported the incident and concluded that "tobacco stemmeries have been warned to discharge negro hands and have complied and many landlords have turned them out. The same policy has been pursued in Lyon County," and the racial violence spread. Raids across the region drove other African Americans from their homes. Political power was at stake: "redeemed" to Democratic rule as early as 1867, white Kentuckians imposed racial segregation in the first decade of the twentieth century. Under Jim Crow laws, African Americans in the tobacco fields faced intimidation and violence, just as they did on the railroads, in streetcars, in public accommodations, and in schoolhouses. This was how local whites prevented the "negro domination" that they feared: through lynchings and assassinations.[40]

Yet, in another retelling of the old Southern story familiar from cotton and sugar production after the war, landowners still needed laborers to grow crops. The president of the first tobacco cooperative in the region said in 1904, "In our country we have an ignorant class of laborers who know nothing except what they learn from us. We white people teach them all they know and take care of them." He also described the dark tobacco cultivation system as "the most slavish crop" he knew, requiring constant effort. Indeed, in 1922, the USDA proved him right. It found that labor requirements for producing dark fire-cured tobacco were evenly distributed across the year, a typical technological choice of slave owners, who had sunk costs in labor and therefore had incentives to make their crews work even in slack seasons.[41] Keeping labor in line through violence, moreover, helped solidify cultivation systems that produced reliable results.

Farmers may have thought that they were creating barriers to entry by pooling leaf in cooperative warehouses and allowing only related commodity producers into their activist societies. Their actions, however, did help define their product as unique. It is not easy to find a reference to the Black Patch as a region producing a unique kind of tobacco before the Black Patch Wars, and the farmers of the affected counties described their tobacco in multitudinous ways for the 1909 census count. Sometimes it was bright and sometimes it was dark, and the many names they called it matched a whole range of cultivation techniques. In this case, the myth of origin indicated that the tobacco type and its technological system of production had always been in place, but little evidence exists to support this point. Instead, the racial violence and agrarian radicalism of the Black Patch Wars represent the historical events that solidified type and technique in ways that could not be changed.[42]

However, the actions of the farmers in the region had results quite the reverse of their intentions: as the product's traits solidified, its production requirements became more malleable, particularly when other growers could produce leaf with the same defining traits (color, taste, etc.). Defining the crop according to its characteristics consequently meant that goods possessing those qualities were interchangeable, which is the crucial definition of a commodity and the hell it can create for its producers. From the colonial era to the early twentieth century, tobacco varietals had helped commodify the crop: in the Black Patch, however, the better that growers met the needs of their buyers, the less flexible became their production methods and the markets for their goods. Once both buyers and growers agreed on desirable qualities, those characteristics could be reproduced elsewhere—more cheaply or more efficiently—in commodity hell. By contrast, those growers who made crops to satisfy specific purposes found themselves with a limited range of buyers, each with precise needs, not competing for the leaf.[43]

Bright Tobacco

Bright Flue-Cured Cigarette Tobacco also first emerged after the war, on the Piedmont border between Virginia and North Carolina, in the region's poorest of sandy soils. The 1880 census, which contained an early typology of the leaf, clearly thought that bright tobacco was new—it was upending land values and making mediocre soil worth more than land that had once been considered fine. Before the Civil War, some folks had used the term *bright* to describe tobacco, but the term referred more to a characteristic than to a formal varietal type. Of course, parts of the burley crop were referred to as "bright," and sometimes the word did not even quite denote a color: an 1861 letter described the tobacco its author sought as "bright (not yellow)."[44] Another writer, from about the same period, called for "a bright mahogany color" or "a rich red color with some brightness." It had been a characteristic of the leaf that was not necessarily tied to seed or soil or the methods that produced it. According to the historical record, nobody cared about those particularities before the war, as long as the tobacco offered had the characteristics the buyer wanted.[45]

Bright tobacco has its own myth of origin, which revolves around Stephen, a slave on a Piedmont plantation that belonged to either Abisha or Elisha Slade. The enslaved man was the "trusted headman" of the plantation, about eighteen years of age, or maybe the plantation blacksmith. The sources contain contradictions. Some say it happened in 1839; others 1840 or 1859. According to most accounts, Stephen was assigned one rainy day to mind fires intended to cure a barn of tobacco. When he fell asleep, the rain put out the fires. On waking, he stoked the fire high in order to cover his mistake. When the barn was opened a few days later, the tobacco had changed color, and the barn contained "six hundred pounds of the brightest yellow tobacco ever seen." This accounts for the characteristic curing method that makes tobacco bright—the adjustment in temperature that helps turn the tobacco toward its characteristic light, bright, and mild traits. Note that the story does not mention flues, however (the ducts that carry the heat of a curing fire throughout the barn while protecting the leaf from the effects of smoke). Some versions of the story say that Stephen used wood, while others say charcoal—and calling him a blacksmith helps account for his access to hotter-burning coal.[46]

Like other examples of the Plantation Illusion, the myth of Bright

Tobacco's origin describes slave society from a postbellum perspective. Stephen's story seems to have made its first appearance after the war, at the same time that the methods that make tobacco bright were solidifying or reaching closure. For example, an 1886 issue of the *Progressive Farmer*, the newspaper of the Farmers' Alliance, a precursor to the 1890s Populist movement, told the tale. The newspaper reported that Stephen, now an old man, made an appearance in a tobacco warehouse where someone recognized him, "pulled off his hat and gave a cheer," which the whole crowd took up, "and the old man grinned all over his face for five minutes." According to this account, "Stephen belonged to Elisha Slade of Caswell, North Carolina. He has always voted the Democratic ticket, and says of his old master, 'I wish he was alive to-day and I was his slave.'" The story of Stephen, which made the technology of producing bright tobacco seem older than it was, also served other purposes. It presented the planter's dream of happy, contented slaves and, by mentioning the Democratic affiliation of its hero—the political party most associated with planters—likewise bolstered the white supremacist politics of the day.[47]

As the story suited a postbellum political ideology that valorized the plantation past, the technological system it intended to explain also fit into the region's emerging political economy. Emancipation had transformed the credit relations of the South. Instead of planters (who had invested capital in the bodies of their workers) seeking credit through commission merchants, now local storekeepers provided the inputs and supplied farmers' needs—and the store expected to be paid at the end of the calendar year. Likewise, sharecropping and tenancy contracts on tobacco plots came to an end in December or January. This new calendar of credit influenced the emerging technological system of Bright Tobacco, just as Kentucky tobacco technology worked to bind laborers to the land. While Stephen's story described the discovery of bright yellow tobacco only in terms of changing the temperature in the curing barn, the system of producing the desirable characteristics eventually comprised not only flue curing but also a distinctive harvest method and a changed marketing system. These new technologies and economic structures derived from the altered historical context—the changing agricultural calendar demanded by the new credit relations—while the calendar and the credit arrangements themselves stemmed from the emancipation of the slaves.[48]

Indeed, the new methods of harvest, curing, and marketing fit into the political economy of emancipation. For example, the new harvest method of Bright Tobacco was called priming, and it involved taking one leaf at a time from the bottom of the plant, as ripeness crept up the stalk. Individual leaves were strung (or looped) onto sticks, which were hung in the barn for curing. Colonial and antebellum growers had usually simply cut down the whole stalk and cured the whole plant, plucking off the leaves afterward. With the priming method of harvesting one leaf at a time, whole systems of production could shift into the new forms wrought by emancipation. The more artisanal, handiwork methods of cultivation, harvest, and curing individual leaves better suited the postbellum scale of production and the freedpeople who made individual arrangements to finance production. After the Civil War, tobacco farms also changed their sizes. They dropped back to tobacco's scale of production from the seventeenth century, before the inspection laws took hold. Smaller farms worked by individual families not only sought credit in local stores, they also sold smaller quantities of leaf, and a new kind of warehouse emerged to market leaf produced on small farms in small quantities.[49]

The new postbellum warehouses were privately owned institutions where buyers and sellers met in auctions that determined the price of small baskets of leaf. Selling baskets of leaf in the warehouse, a few hundred pounds at a time, fit well with the new harvest and curing methods, which filled each barn with leaves that had grown at about the same place on each plant, leaves similar in size and shape. When cured together, under the same conditions, these leaves possessed about the same color and aroma. This made grading and marketing go faster. What had been an eighteen-month crop in the colonial period tightened into very nearly an annual production cycle, which again suited the credit needs of the emancipated workforce. The new harvest and curing techniques helped this transformation. In the Kentucky areas producing Dark Fire-Cured Tobacco and in the Bright

Flue-Cured Tobacco region, the new technologies suited particular responses to the changes that came out of the Civil War. The tobacco types codified by the USDA in 1925 expressed this transformation. They were produced with specific techniques in particular regions, and these techniques made leaf with distinctive characteristics demanded by particular markets. The tobacco types date from this period, from the political economies of particular regions. Political economy provided the key context for technological change.[50]

Tracing Techniques to Their Conclusion

One final example punctuates the point: Perique tobacco is a type grown on only two hills that rise above the swampland of St. James Parish in Louisiana. In 1880, it was still harvested in ways developed in eighteenth-century French colonies: plucking individual leaves as soon as the second-growth suckers appeared. It was cured under successive applications of pressure, which squeezed out the juices until it shone with an oily blackness, and it was marketed in carottes. The persistence of these unique harvesting, curing, and marketing methods indicates the importance of institutions in shaping market relations. It demonstrates a tobacco technology that developed far from the inspection laws of the English Chesapeake. Perique became a tobacco type—as clearly marked by its cultivation system as are the types of Virginia and Kentucky. In 1971, it took four or five years for Perique to move from seedbed to final sale, and merchants paid the growing and processing costs for farmers, supervised the final stages of curing and handling, and told the farmers how much to grow. Merchants based their assessments of market size on their similarly close relationship with manufacturers of pipe tobacco blends and a few other specialty markets.[51]

These long-standing trade connections provided the basis for market regulation disguised as botanic taxonomy. Clearly, tobacco types cannot be explained entirely by genetics. The historical record, however, provides obvious if complicated explanations. The Dark Fire-Cured Tobacco of Kentucky and Tennessee enters mostly African markets, while Bright Flue-Cured Tobacco became an important part of the emerging emphasis on cigarette manufacturing. Perique Tobacco of Louisiana, first developed in the French colonies, is still produced with methods from the eighteenth century that took shape in a specific relationship between producer and buyer, and a regulatory environment distinct from the English coast and its inspection laws. These tobacco types do not come from the seeds. They are a form of economic regulation that grew out of long-standing trade relationships and the various institutional environments that shaped those interactions. Negotiations between buyers and sellers and the merchants who mediated between them resulted in distinctive characteristics for leaf grown in specific regions, traits eventually produced with specific technologies likewise specific to their regions. As the USDA attempts to help farmers meet their markets more precisely today, it tells them how to grow their commodified products to best satisfy the needs of the buyers. These characteristics look like nature, but they are technologies instead. Like every other staple crop in this book, humans defined tobacco into commodities, global products with complex human histories.

RICHARD FOLLETT

Conclusion

❧

TRAVEL THE BACK ROADS of the rural South, and the legacies of America's plantation kingdoms are still visible. Cotton patches on US 80 west of Demopolis, Alabama; a rich stand of sugar cane in Iberville Parish, Louisiana; tobacco leaves fluttering alongside the road to Courtland, Virginia; and a rice mill in Crowley, Louisiana—eight hundred miles west of where the colonial rice industry began. Today, farmers precision grade sugar fields, harvest rice with mechanical combines, and grow genetically modified cotton. Technology and know-how still enables American farmers to compete in ferociously competitive global markets, but the slow outmigration from Southern farming continues as diversification eliminates the last remnants of the monocropped plantation complex. Catfish ponds and poultry farms all too often stand on the land once made rich by the labor of enslaved African Americans, and even in the heart of Dixie, soybeans, peanuts, corn, and wheat grow alongside cotton.

Modern production techniques still produce sizeable cotton crops even in the lower South, but the region's privileged position in domestic and international markets was eclipsed long ago. In 2013, Alabama produced 585,000 bales, or 4.5 percent of all US ginned cotton. On the eve of the Civil War, enslaved workers in Demopolis and Alabama's so-called black belt picked almost 990,000 bales in the state; it was a giant crop that supplied 22 percent of all cotton shipped to Britain,

Continental Europe, and the rest of the United States.[1] Once the epicenter of a vast global cotton empire, Demopolis today is a quiet Southern town, a relative backwater, its once-busy wharves along the Black Warrior and Tombigbee Rivers now empty. The indomitable Greek Revival plantation houses still attract their visitors, but the grinding legacies of slavery and the struggle for freedom in Alabama's cotton heartland is never far removed.

"Cotton fields no more," wrote the distinguished Southern historian Gilbert Fite in 1984. Kudzu—an invasive weed introduced to the United States from Asia in 1876—has replaced cotton as the South's most distinctive plant, and at its current rate of growth, 150,000 acres annually, the pea-like vine will literally smother parts of the Southern landscape within the space of a few decades. It is a cruel but fitting irony that an Asian weed should vanquish Georgia and Alabama, covering the relics of the nineteenth-century past beneath a thick carpet of leaves and vines. Kudzu is not the first, nor possibly the last, Asian import to wreak havoc on the Southern countryside. As this book makes clear, Indian cotton, Chinese rice, and Philippine sugar dethroned the once powerful plantation kingdoms of the American South. Today, Brazil, India, and China jostle for the top places in the world's sugar, tobacco, and cotton league tables; Indonesia and Bangladesh join the big two Asian nations as global rice leaders. The United States places third in global cotton production, though the widespread adoption of genetically modified cotton in India and neighboring Pakistan will undoubtedly test the resilience of US cotton growers once again.[2]

American farmers are not new to foreign competition. From the earliest days of colonial Virginia to the present, global markets have profoundly shaped Southern life and labor. Racial slavery and the plantation system served white Southerners well, enriching many and insulating others from open competition with the region's African American population. By contrast, "life in thraldom"—as the early Southern historian Ulrich B. Phillips called it—was nasty, brutish, and long for those tragically enslaved, and the word *tragic* is employed here not blithely, as the contemporary media is wont to do, but soberly and deliberately. Slavery was indeed tragic for those in chains, but, as these chapters have underscored, it also proved to be phenomenally profitable for those who owned the land, enslaved people, financial capital, steamboats, foundries, supply yards, banks, insurance agents, cotton mills, and on and on. Cotton export receipts additionally filled the government's coffers. No wonder then that Senator James Henry Hammond bullishly called it "King Cotton" in 1858.[3]

A decade later, America's plantation kingdoms lay in ruins, its slaves emancipated, and its once powerful slaveholders bankrupted. The postwar economy provided a feeble base for economic reconstruction. With no land granted them during the postwar emancipation settlement, formerly enslaved African Americans toiled as a waged proletariat in Louisiana's sugar fields, sharecropped cotton patches from the Carolinas to Texas, and entered into contract labor agreements in the rice districts, while, in the Virginia tobacco fields, black sharecropping and white tenancy edged forward. Southern elites underwent a transition themselves, moving from prewar labor lords to postwar landlords, but the severe shortage of capital, the dispersal of plantation production to small farms, and the downsizing of production units left the plantation complex a shadow of its former self. Enmeshed in a culture of tenancy, sharecropping, and, from the 1890s, racial segregation and voter disenfranchisement, Southern farmers marched down a debilitating road that delayed the region's growth and relegated it to the status of a developing-world agricultural colony. As Marxist historian Eric Hobsbawm concluded, these choices left the American South "agrarian, poor, backward, and resentful," in direct counterpoint to the "dramatic speed and impressiveness" of Northern industrialization. Enfeebled by race, reunion, and a culture of conservative authoritarianism, landholders throughout the Southern states were structurally and ideologically ill equipped to tackle the onslaught of global economic competition. As the preceding chapters indicate, some Southern producers struggled to maintain a competitive advantage, but whether in rice, cotton, sugar, or tobacco, the road to economic perdition and commodity hell lay ahead.[4]

World markets have always been axiomatic to Southern economic and social development. They were the midwives at the American

South's birthing, yet over time global competition—the wellspring of the early South—humbled the region's erstwhile plantation kingdoms. Outproduced by cheaper and sometimes more efficient competitors, Southern producers nonetheless found in memory, film, and popular music a "usable," albeit fictive, past that restored Dixie's "Land of Cotton" to its former greatness. Throughout the twentieth century, moviegoing audiences rekindled the memory of rich cotton fields—divorced from reality—in the Hollywood blockbuster *Gone with the Wind*, while more recently the country music band Alabama evoked the most iconic of lyrics, giving voice to the enduing power of cotton and the American South's global plantation commodities.

> We were walkin' in high cotton
> Old times there are not forgotten
> Those fertile fields are never far away.[5]

NOTES

❦

Introduction

1. *Selections from the Letters and Speeches of the Hon. James H. Hammond, of South Carolina* (New York: John F. Trow, 1866), 311–322.

2. Lewis Cecil Gray, *History of Agriculture in the Southern United States to 1860*, 2 vols. (Washington, DC: Carnegie Institution of Washington, 1933) 2:693; Richard Follett, *The Sugar Masters: Planters and Slaves in Louisiana's Cane World, 1820–1860* (Baton Rouge: Louisiana State University, 2005); Helen Taylor, *Circling Dixie: Contemporary Southern Culture through a Transatlantic Lens* (New Brunswick, NJ: Rutgers University Press, 2001), 28–62.

3. Russell R. Menard, "Slave Demography in the Low Country, 1670–1740: From Frontier Society to Plantation Regime," *South Carolina Historical Magazine* 96 (October 1995): 284; Philip D. Morgan, *Slave Counterpoint: Black Culture in the Eighteenth-Century Chesapeake and Lowcountry* (Chapel Hill: University of North Carolina, 1998), 61, 63; "AHR Exchange: The Question of 'Black Rice,'" *American Historical Review* 115 (February 2010): 123–171; Peter A. Coclanis, *The Shadow of a Dream: Economic Life and Death in the South Carolina Low Country, 1670–1920* (New York: Oxford University Press, 1989), 64, 82, 85; S. Max Edelson, *Plantation Enterprise in Colonial South Carolina* (Cambridge, MA: Harvard University Press, 2006), 83–85.

4. Gerald David Jaynes, *Branches without Roots: Genesis of the Black Working Class in the American South, 1862–1882* (New York: Oxford University Press, 1986), 35; Gavin Wright, *The Political Economy of the Cotton South: Households, Markets, and Wealth in the Nineteenth Century* (New York: W. W. Norton, 1978), 25–29, 90–97; Brian Schoen, *The Fragile Fabric of Union: Cotton, Federal Politics, and the Global Origins of the Civil War* (Baltimore: Johns Hopkins University Press, 2010).

5. Scott P. Marler, *The Merchants' Capital: New Orleans and the Political Economy of the Nineteenth Century South* (Cambridge: Cambridge University Press, 2013), 226–228; Eric Foner, *Reconstruction: America's Unfinished Revolution, 1863–1877*

(New York: HarperCollins, 1988); Richard Holcombe Kilbourne, *Debt, Investment, Slaves: Credit Relations in East Feliciana Parish, Louisiana, 1825–1885* (Tuscaloosa: University of Alabama Press, 1995), 7–8.

6. L. Diane Barnes, Brian Schoen, and Frank Towers, eds., *The Old South's Modern Worlds: Slavery, Region, and Nation in the Age of Progress* (New York: Oxford University Press, 2011), 10, 305; Walter Johnson, *Rivers of Dark Dreams: Slavery and Empire in the Cotton Kingdom* (Cambridge, MA: Harvard University Press, 2013), 254; Edward E. Baptist, *The Half Has Never Been Told: Slavery and the Making of American Capitalism* (New York: Basic Books, 2014), 112–15, 135, 141; Sven Beckert, *Empire of Cotton: A Global History* (New York: Alfred A. Knopf, 2014), 107, 111; Seth Rockman and Sven Beckert, eds., *Slavery's Capitalism: A New History of American Economic Development* (Philadelphia: University of Pennsylvania Press, forthcoming).

7. Marx quoted in Roger Ransom and Richard Sutch, "Capitalists without Capital: Slavery and the Impact of Emancipation," *Agricultural History* 62 (Summer 1988): 133; Christopher Morris, *The Big Muddy: An Environmental History of the Mississippi and Its Peoples* (New York: Oxford University Press, 2012), 116–118; D. B. Allen to "Dear Mother," November 13, 1851, D. B. Allen letter, Mss. 3572, Louisiana and Lower Mississippi Valley Collection, LSU Libraries, Baton Rouge, LA, quoted in Carin Peller Semmens, "Unreconstructed: Slavery and Emancipation on Louisiana's Red River" (PhD diss., University of Sussex, 2015), 1.

8. Dale Tomich, *Through the Prism of Slavery: Labor, Control, and World Economy* (Lanham, MD: Rowman and Littlefield, 2004), 56–71; Dale Tomich and Michael Zeuske, "The Second Slavery: Mass Slavery, World Economy and Comparative Microhistories," *Review: A Journal of the Fernand Braudel Center* 31 (2008): 91–100; Anthony Kaye, "The Second Slavery: Modernity in the Nineteenth-Century South and the Atlantic World," *Journal of Southern History* 75 (August 2009): 627.

9. Alan L. Olmstead and Paul W. Rhode, *Creating Abundance: Biological Innovation and American Agricultural Development* (Cambridge: Cambridge University Press, 2008).

10. Gavin Wright, *Old South, New South: Revolutions in the Southern Economy since the Civil War* (New York: Basic Books, 1986); Richard Follett, Eric Foner, and Walter Johnson, *Slavery's Ghost: The Problem of Freedom in the Age of Emancipation* (Baltimore: Johns Hopkins University Press, 2011), 61.

11. Alex Lichtenstein, "Rethinking Agrarian Labor in the U.S. South," *Journal of Peasant Studies* 35 (October 2008): 632.

The Road to Commodity Hell

1. John Locke, *Further Considerations Concerning Raising the Value of Money . . .* (London: Printed for Awnsham and John Churchill, 1695), 21.

2. On the first appearance of the term in English, see the *Oxford English Dictionary*. The Common Era (CE) dates times from the alleged birth of Jesus Christ until now.

3. Karl Marx, *A Contribution to the Critique of Political Economy*, ed. Maurice Dobb (New York: International, 1970; originally published in German in 1859), 28.

4. Ulrike Schaede, "Forwards and Futures in Tokugawa-Period Japan: A New Perspective on the Dōjima Rice Market," *Journal of Banking and Finance* 13 (September 1989): 487–513; Shigeru Wakita, "Efficiency of the Dōjima Rice Futures Market in Tokugawa-Period Japan," *Journal of Banking and Finance* 25 (March 2001): 535–554; David A. Moss and Eugene Kintgen, *The Dōjima Rice Market and the Origins of Futures Trading*, Harvard Business School Case Study, no. 709044 (Boston: Harvard Business School, 2009); Kara Newman, *The Secret Financial Life of Food: From Commodities Markets to Supermarkets* (New York: Columbia University Press, 2013), 6.

5. See, for example, Peter A. Coclanis, "Distant Thunder: The Creation of a World Market in Rice and the Transformations It Wrought," *American Historical Review* 98 (October 1993): 1050–1078; Coclanis, "The Rice Industry of the United States," in *Rice: Origin, Antiquity and History*, ed. S. D. Sharma (Enfield, NH: Science / CRC Press, Taylor & Francis Group, 2010), 411–431; Coclanis, "White Rice: The Midwestern Origins of the Modern Rice Industry in the United States," in *Rice: A Global History*, ed. Francesca Bray, Peter A. Coclanis, Edda Fields-Black, and Dagmar Schäfer (Cambridge: Cambridge University Press, 2015), 291–317.

6. See the works cited in the previous note.

7. Coclanis, "Rice Industry of the United States," in Sharma, *Rice*, 411–412; Coclanis, "White Rice," in Bray et al., *Rice*; J. L. Maclean, D. C. Dawe, B. Hardy, and G. P. Hettel, eds., *Rice Almanac: Source Book for the Most Important Economic Activity on Earth*, 3rd ed. (Los Baños, Philippines: International Rice Research Institute, 2002), 6–8.

8. See, for example, S. D. Sharma, "Domestication and Diaspora of Rice," in Sharma, *Rice*, 1–24; Coclanis, "White Rice," in Bray et al., *Rice*.

9. See Peter A. Coclanis, "Rice Prices in the 1720s and the Evolution of the South Carolina Economy," *Journal of Southern History* 48 (November 1982): 531–544; Coclanis, *The Shadow of a Dream: Economic Life and Death in the South Carolina Low Country, 1670–1920* (New York: Oxford University Press, 1989), 61–63; Coclanis, "Distant Thunder," 1053–1055; Coclanis, "White Rice," in Bray et al., *Rice*; Maclean et al., *Rice Almanac*, 1–9; Nathan Childs, *2010/11 Rice Yearbook*, RCS-2012 (Washington, DC: US Department of Agriculture, Economic Research Service, April 2012), 3–7. On the concept of iatrogenesis and iatrogenic illness, see, for example, Ivan Illich, *Medical Nemesis: The Expropriation of Health* (New York: Pantheon, 1976); Virginia A. Sharpe and Alan I. Faden, *Medical Harm: Historical, Con-*

ceptual, and Ethical Dimensions of Iatrogenic Illness (Cambridge: Cambridge University Press, 1998).

10. Coclanis, "Rice Prices in the 1720s and the Evolution of the South Carolina Economy"; Coclanis, *Shadow of a Dream*, 61–63.

11. See, for example, Judith A. Carney, "From Hands to Tutors: African Expertise in the South Carolina Rice Economy," *Agricultural History* 67 (Summer 1993): 1–30; Carney, *Black Rice: The African Origins of Rice Cultivation in the Americas* (Cambridge, MA: Harvard University Press, 2001); Carney and Richard Nicholas Rosomoff, *In the Shadow of Slavery: Africa's Botanical Legacy in the Atlantic World* (Berkeley: University of California Press, 2009), 150–154 and passim. For alternative views, see Peter A. Coclanis, "How the Low Country Was Taken to Task: Slave-Labor Organization in Coastal South Carolina and Georgia," in *Slavery, Secession, and Southern History*, ed. Robert Louis Paquette and Louis Ferleger (Charlottesville: University Press of Virginia, 2000), 59–78; David Eltis, Philip D. Morgan, and David Richardson, "Agency and Diaspora in Atlantic History: Reassessing the African Contribution to Rice Cultivation in the Americas," *American Historical Review* 112 (December 2007): 1329–1358; Coclanis, "White Rice," in Bray et al., *Rice*. Cantillon lays out his view regarding the risk-bearing function of entrepreneurship in his *Essay on the Nature of Commerce in General* (New Brunswick, NJ: Transaction, 2001; originally published in French in 1755).

12. See, for example, Lewis Cecil Gray, *History of Agriculture in the Southern United States to 1860*, 2 vols. (Washington, DC: Carnegie Institution of Washington, 1933; repr. ed., Gloucester, MA: Peter Smith, 1958), 1:277–284; Peter A. Coclanis, "Rice," in *The South Carolina Encyclopedia*, ed. Walter B. Edgar (Columbia: University of South Carolina Press, 2006), 791–794; S. Max Edelson, *Plantation Enterprise in Colonial South Carolina* (Cambridge, MA: Harvard University Press, 2006), 53–125.

13. Estimated from data in Coclanis, "Rice Industry of the United States," in Sharma, *Rice*, 415; V. D. Wickizer and M. K. Bennett, *The Rice Economy of Monsoon Asia* (Palo Alto, CA: Food Research Institute, Stanford University, 1941), 31–37; D. H. Grist, *Rice*, 3rd ed. (London: Longmans, Green, 1959), 348–358; Randolph Barker, Robert W. Herdt, with Beth Rose, *The Rice Economy of Asia*, 2 vols. (Washington, DC: Resources for the Future, 1985), 1:42–46; Maclean et al., *Rice Almanac*, 4–6.

14. See Gray, *History of Agriculture*, 1:279–284; Coclanis, *Shadow of a Dream*, 96–98; Joyce E. Chaplin, *An Anxious Pursuit: Agricultural Innovation and Modernity in the Lower South, 1730–1815* (Chapel Hill: University of North Carolina Press, 1993), 227–276; Coclanis, "Rice," in Edgar, *South Carolina Encyclopedia*, 791–794; Edelson, *Plantation Enterprise*, 103–113. On the development of the rice industry in the Georgia low country, see Julia Floyd Smith, *Slavery and Rice Culture in Low Country Georgia, 1750–1860* (Knoxville: University of Tennessee Press, 1985), esp. 15–63; Mart A. Stewart, *"What Nature Suffers to Groe": Life, Labor, and Landscape on*

the Georgia Coastal Plain, 1680–1920 (Athens: University of Georgia Press, 1996), esp. 98–114; Peter A. Coclanis, "Rice," in *The New Georgia Encyclopedia,* ed. John C. Inscoe (Athens: University of Georgia Press, 2004), http://www.georgiaencyclopedia.org/nge/Article.jsp?id=h-899.

15. See Coclanis, "How the Low Country Was Taken to Task"; Peter A. Coclanis, "The Economics of Slavery," in *The Oxford Handbook of Slavery in the Americas,* ed. Robert Paquette and Mark M. Smith (New York: Oxford University Press, 2010), 489–512.

16. Coclanis, *Shadow of a Dream,* 63–110, 121–130; Alice Hanson Jones, *Wealth of a Nation to Be: The American Colonies on the Eve of the Revolution* (New York: Columbia University Press, 1980), 357.

17. Coclanis, *Shadow of a Dream,* 121–130; Lee Soltow, *Men and Wealth in the United States, 1850–1870* (New Haven, CT: Yale University Press, 1975), 101, 166–167, 195n6; William Kauffman Scarborough, *Masters of the Big House: Elite Slaveholders of the Mid-nineteenth-Century South* (Baton Rouge: Louisiana State University Press, 2003), passim; Adam Rothman, "The 'Slave Power' in the United States, 1783–1865," in *Ruling America: A History of Wealth and Power in a Democracy,* ed. Gary Gerstle and Steve Fraser (Cambridge: Harvard University Press, 2005), 64–91, 307–315, esp. pp. 71–73.

18. Coclanis, *Shadow of a Dream,* 112, 142; Stewart, *"What Nature Suffers to Groe,"* appendix, 253–257; John C. Inscoe, "Georgia in 1860," in Inscoe, *New Georgia Encyclopedia.*

19. Coclanis, *Shadow of a Dream,* 84–91, 121–130, 149–154; Dale Evans Swan, *The Structure and Profitability of the Antebellum Rice Industry 1859* (New York: Arno Press, 1975), 15. On the high levels of inequality in the South more generally, see Soltow, *Men and Wealth in the United States, 1850–1870,* 92–123. For a superb study of the yeomanry in the low country, see Stephanie McCurry, *Masters of Small Worlds: Yeoman Households, Gender Relations, and the Political Culture of the Antebellum South Carolina Low Country* (New York: Oxford University Press, 1995).

20. See Scarborough, *Masters of the Big House,* 9, 12–13, appendixes A, B, C, D, 427–484; Peter A. Coclanis, introduction to *Seed from Madagascar,* by Duncan Heyward (Columbia: University of South Carolina Press, 1993; originally published 1937), ix–l, esp. xxii–xxiii; Coclanis, introduction to *Twilight on the South Carolina Rice Fields: Letters of the Heyward Family 1862–1871,* ed. Margaret Belser Hollis and Allen H. Stokes (Columbia: University of South Carolina Press, 2010), xvii–xxxi, esp. xviii. The value in 2013 of Nathaniel Heyward's estate—valued at $2,018,000 at the time of his death in April 1851—was calculated via the site Measuring Worth, http://www.measuringworth.com/uscompare/.

21. Scarborough, *Masters of the Big House,* appendixes A ,B, C, D, 427–484; Coclanis, introduction to Heyward, *Seed from Madagascar,* ix–l.

22. See, for example, Coclanis, *Shadow of a Dream*, 48–158; Smith, *Slavery and Rice Culture in Low Country Georgia, 1750–1860*, 15–44.

23. Swan, *Structure and Profitability of the Antebellum Rice Industry 1859*, 87–89, 104–112.

24. Ibid., 87–89, 104–112; James Oakes, *The Ruling Race: A History of American Slaveholders* (New York: Alfred A. Knopf, 1982), 37–68, 245–250.

25. Coclanis, "Distant Thunder," 1050–1054; Andrew M. Watson, *Agricultural Innovation in the Early Islamic World: The Diffusion of Crops and Farming Techniques, 700–1100* (Cambridge: Cambridge University Press, 1983); Michael Decker, "Plants and Progress: Rethinking the Islamic Agricultural Revolution," *Journal of World History* 20 (June 2009): 187–206, esp. 194–197; Peiraldo Bullio, "Problemi e geografia della risicoltura in Piemonte nei secoli XVII e XVIII," *Annali della Fondazione Luigi Einaudi* 3 (1969): 37–93; Luigi Faccini, *L'economia risicola lombarda dagli inizi del XVIII secolo all'Unità* (Milan: SugarCo, 1976), 23–26; Elda Gentili Zappi, *If Eight Hours Seem Too Few: Mobilization of Women Workers in the Italian Rice Fields* (Albany: State University of New York Press, 1991), 1–33; Maclean et al., *Rice Almanac*, 4–6; Aldo Ferrero and Francesco Vidotto, "History of Rice in Europe," in Sharma, *Rice*, 341–372.

26. Coclanis, *Shadow of a Dream*, 13–26, 48–63, 133–135; Coclanis, "Distant Thunder," 1050–1062; Coclanis, "Rice Industry of the United States," in Sharma, *Rice*, 419–420, 429; David Henley, "Rizification Revisited: Re-Examining the Rise of Rice in Indonesia with Special Reference to Sulawesi," in *Smallholders and Stockbreeders: History of Foodcrop and Livestock Farming in Southeast Asia*, ed. Peter Boomgaard and David Henley (Leiden: KITLV Press, 2004), 107–138; Sui-wai Cheung, "A Desire to Eat Well: Rice and the Market in Eighteenth-Century China," in Bray et al., *Rice*, 84–98.

27. Coclanis, "Distant Thunder," 1051–1053; R. C. Nash, "South Carolina and the Atlantic Economy in the Late Seventeenth and Eighteenth Centuries," *Economic History Review*, n.s., 45 (November 1992): 677–702; Coclanis, "Rice Industry of the United States," in Sharma, *Rice*, 419–420, 429.

28. Coclanis, "Distant Thunder," 1051–1053; Nash, "South Carolina and the Atlantic Economy," esp. 680–682; Thomas L. Haskell, "Capitalism and the Origins of the Humanitarian Sensibility," *American Historical Review* 90 (April 1985): 339–361 and 90 (June 1985): 547–566. On the tendency for nation-states to "buy environment" as they grow wealthier, see, for example, Bjørn Lomborg, *Cool It: The Skeptical Environmentalist's Guide to Global Warming* (New York: Random House, 2007), 47–52, 149–151.

29. John Marshall, *Principles of Economics*, 8th ed. (London: Macmillan, 1920), book 3, chapter 6, paragraph 17, Library of Economics and Liberty website, http://www.econlib.org/library/Marshall/marP14.html#Bk.III,Ch.VI; Robert T. Jensen

and Nolan H. Miller, "Giffen Behavior and Subsistence Consumption," *American Economic Review* 98 (September 2008): 1553–1577.

30. Coclanis, "Distant Thunder," 1051–1062; Nash, "South Carolina and the Atlantic Economy," 681–702.

31. Coclanis, "Distant Thunder," 1051–1062; Nash, "South Carolina and the Atlantic Economy," 681–702; Peter A. Coclanis, "Southeast Asia's Incorporation into the World Rice Market: A Revisionist View," *Journal of Southeast Asian Studies* 24 (September 1993): 251–267.

32. Coclanis, *Shadow of a Dream*, esp. 61–110. For the sources of the statistics in the text regarding increasing concentration of slaveholdings in St. Johns Berkeley Parish, see pp. 98, 259. *Ghost acres* is a term coined in the 1960s denoting external, often underpopulated lands that can be utilized by a given area or country for additional "carrying capacity," thereby easing "land" (natural resource) constraints and allowing for additional economic production, surplus extraction, etc. Some scholars in recent years have argued that the Americas after 1492 served such a function for Europe. For one inspired attempt to employ the concept in such a way, see Kenneth Pomeranz, *The Great Divergence: China, Europe, and the Making of the Modern World Economy* (Princeton, NJ: Princeton University Press, 2000), 264–297.

33. Coclanis, *Shadow of a Dream*, 111–158; Coclanis, "Distant Thunder," 1056–1078.

34. Bernard Bailyn, "The Challenge of Modern Historiography," *American Historical Review* 87 (February 1982): 1–24 (quote appears on p. 10).

35. Coclanis, *Shadow of a Dream*, 48–158; Coclanis, "Distant Thunder."

36. Coclanis, *Shadow of a Dream*, 130–154; Coclanis, "Distant Thunder," 1056–1057; Peter A. Coclanis, "The Poetics of American Agriculture: The U.S. Rice Industry in International Perspective," *Agricultural History* 69 (Spring 1995): 140–162.

37. Coclanis, *Shadow of a Dream*, 135–137; Coclanis, "Distant Thunder," 1056–1070; Coclanis, "Southeast Asia's Incorporation into the World Rice Market." The quote in the text from David Macpherson is from his famous work, *Annals of Commerce, Manufactures, Fisheries, and Navigation*, 4 vols. (London: Nichols and Son, 1805), 4:362.

38. See the works cited in the previous note. Also see Dauril Alden, "The Growth and Decline of Indigo Production in Colonial Brazil: A Study in Comparative Economic History," *Journal of Economic History* 25 (March 1965): 35–60.

39. Coclanis, *Shadow of a Dream*, 133–142; Coclanis, "Distant Thunder"; Coclanis, "White Rice," in Bray et al., *Rice*.

40. Coclanis, "Distant Thunder"; Coclanis, "White Rice," in Bray et al., *Rice*; Arthur H. Cole, "The American Rice-Growing Industry: A Study of Comparative Advantage," *Quarterly Journal of Economics* 41 (August 1927): 595–643.

41. Peter A. Coclanis, "Bitter Harvest: The South Carolina Low Country in

Historical Perspective," *Journal of Economic History* 45 (June 1985): 251–259; Cocla-nis, "The Rise and Fall of the South Carolina Low Country: An Essay in Economic Interpretation," *Southern Studies* 24 (Summer 1985): 143–166; John Komlos and Peter A. Coclanis, "Time in the Paddies: A Comparison of Rice Production in the Southeastern United States and Lower Burma in the Nineteenth Century," *Social Science History* 11 (Fall 1987): 343–354; Coclanis, *Shadow of a Dream*, 130–143; Cocla-nis, "Southeast Asia's Incorporation into the World Rice Market"; Coclanis, "Po-etics of American Agriculture"; Coclanis, "Rice Industry of the United States," in Sharma, *Rice*; Coclanis, "White Rice," in Bray et al., *Rice*. In his excellent recent study of the decline and fall of the rice industry in South Carolina, James H. Tuten, for example, incorporates international developments—i.e., Asian competition—into his argument. See Tuten, *Lowcountry Time and Tide: The Fall of the South Carolina Rice Kingdom* (Columbia: University of South Carolina Press, 2010).

42. See Coclanis, *Shadow of a Dream*, 140–141; Swan, *Structure and Profitability of the Antebellum Rice Industry 1859*, preface, esp. 75–84. On the possibility that by the late antebellum period rice plantations in the low country had become rather more platforms for raising slaves than viable agricultural operations, see Jeffrey Doyle Richardson, "Nothing More Fruitful: Debt and Cash Flow on the Antebel-lum Rice Plantation" (master's thesis, University of North Carolina–Chapel Hill, 1995).

43. See Coclanis, "Southeast Asia's Integration into the World Rice Market"; Coclanis, "Distant Thunder."

44. See Komlos and Coclanis, "Time in the Paddies"; Coclanis, "Distant Thun-der," 1062–1072. Regarding Marx and "windfalls," see Karl Marx, *Capital*, ed. Fred-erick Engels, trans. Samuel Moore and Edward Aveling, 3 vols. (New York: Interna-tional, 1967; originally published 1867–1894), 1:750–754. P. P. Rey and Giovanni Arrighi are perhaps the two scholars most closely associated with the "articulation of production modes" approach, and Paul Richards and Harro Maat of Wagenin-gen University in the Netherlands have recently been developing a research pro-gram around the "anticommodity" theme. Hla Myint's interpretation is outlined in two essays, each more than a half century old, but still well worth reading. See Myint, "The Gains from International Trade and the Backward Countries," *Review of Economic Studies* 22, no. 2 (1954–1955): 129–142; Myint, "The 'Classical Theory' of International Trade and the Underdeveloped Countries," *Economic Journal* 68 (June 1958): 317–337.

45. Gray, *History of Agriculture*, 2:725–726. On the price differentials in Europe—in Liverpool and Rotterdam to be more specific—between "Carolina" rice and East Indian rice in the 1820s, see, for example, the collection of "Prices Current" in the Enoch Silsby Papers, Southern Historical Collection, University of North Carolina-Chapel Hill, Chapel Hill, NC. The "Prices-Current at Rotterdam,"

dated July 19, 1821, shows Carolina rice trading at $3.50 per hundredweight, Bengal rice at $2.50, and Java rice at $2.25. The "Prices Current" at Liverpool, dated December 2, 1826, has Carolina rice trading at 20s.–23s. [shillings] per hundredweight, with Bengal rice selling at 19s.–21s. (white) and 18s.–19s. (yellow). Note, too, that American rice faced duties of an additional 15s. per hundredweight, while Bengal rice, enjoying an imperial preference, faced duties of only 5s. per hundredweight. The "Prices Current" at Liverpool, dated January 19, 1828, has "old" Carolina rice selling at 17s.–20s. per hundredweight and Bengal rice selling at 15s.–16s.-6d. per hundredweight (white) and 13s.–14s.-6d. per hundredweight (yellow). At that time, the duty on American rice was still 15s. per hundredweight, but the duty on Indian rice had been reduced further to 4s. per hundredweight. The quote in the text regarding the perceived quality of Carolina rice is from Duncan Heyward. See his *Seed from Madagascar*, 4. Rice from the United States was considered by Westerners to be of higher quality than rice imported from India and the East Indies. See, for example, H. J. S. Cotton, "The Rice Trade of the World," *Calcutta Review* 58 (1874): 267–302. The quote in the text from David Doar is from his *Rice and Rice Planting in the South Carolina Low Country* (Charleston, SC: Charleston Museum, 1936), 42.

46. Coclanis, *Shadow of a Dream*, 128–158; Tuten, *Lowcountry Time and Tide*, 32–74; Stewart, *"What Nature Suffers to Groe,"* 193–242. For an important new study of the phosphate and fertilizer industries in the low country, see Shepherd W. McKinley, *Stinking Stones and Rocks of Gold: Phosphate, Fertilizer, and Industrialization in Postbellum South Carolina* (Gainesville: University Press of Florida, 2014). On the business concept "commodity hell," see, for example, Oren Harari, *Break from the Pack: How to Compete in a Copycat Economy* (Upper Saddle River, NJ: FT Press, 2006), esp. 15–36; Richard D'Aveni, *Beating the Commodity Trap: How to Maximize Your Competitive Position and Increase Your Pricing Power* (Boston: Harvard Business School Press, 2010). Note that the pattern found in the South Atlantic rice region—early wealth followed by protracted economic decline—has been traced in other areas colonized by European powers. See, for example, Daron Acemoglu, Simon Johnson, and James A. Robinson, "Reversal of Fortune: Geography and Institutions in the Making of the Modern World Income Distribution," *Quarterly Journal of Economics* 117 (November 2002): 1231–1294.

47. Andrew Holmes, *Commoditization and the Strategic Response* (Aldershot, UK: Gower, 2008), 5.

48. Pete Daniel, *Breaking the Land: The Transformation of Cotton, Tobacco, and Rice Cultures since 1880* (Urbana: University of Illinois Press, 1985), 39–61, 134–151, 215–236, 271–289; Henry C. Dethloff, *A History of the American Rice Industry, 1685–1985* (College Station: Texas A&M University Press, 1988), 63–194; Coclanis, "White Rice," in Bray et al., *Rice*.

Cotton and the US South

1. For a fuller exploration of these topics, see Sven Beckert, *Empire of Cotton: A Global History* (New York: Alfred A. Knopf, 2014). This chapter draws on and uses material from *Empire of Cotton*.

2. Sven Beckert, "Emancipation and Empire: Reconstructing the Worldwide Web of Cotton Production in the Age of the American Civil War," *American Historical Review* 109 (December 2004): 1405–1438.

3. John Greenleaf Whittier, "The Hashish," *John Greenleaf Whittier: Selected Poems*, ed. Brenda Wineapple (New York: Library of America, 2004), 43–44.

4. Beckert, *Empire of Cotton*, 102; Sven Beckert, "Slavery and Capitalism," *Chronicle of Higher Education*, December 12, 2014; Beckert, "Emancipation and Empire," 1408.

5. J. T. Danson, "On the Existing Connection between American Slavery and the British Cotton Manufacture," *Journal of the Statistical Society of London* 20 (March 1857): 7. For a similar argument, see Élisée Reclus, "Le coton et la crise américaine," *Revue des Deux Mondes* 37 (January 1862): 176, 187. Herman Merivale, *Lectures on Colonization and Colonies, Delivered before the University of Oxford in 1839, 1840 & 1841* (repr., London: Humphrey Milford, 1928), 301–302.

6. United States Department of Commerce and Bureau of the Census, *Historical Statistics of the United States, Colonial Times to 1970*, Part 1 (Washington, DC: Government Printing Office, 1975), 518; Edward Baines, *History of the Cotton Manufacture in Great Britain* (London: H. Fisher, R. Fisher, and P. Jackson, 1835), 302; Michael M. Edwards, *The Growth of the British Cotton Trade, 1780–1815* (Manchester: Manchester University Press, 1967), 89.

7. Joyce E. Chaplin, *An Anxious Pursuit: Agricultural Innovation and Modernity in the Lower South, 1730–1815* (Chapel Hill: University of North Carolina Press, 1993), 220–226.

8. Stuart W. Bruchey, *Cotton and the Growth of the American Economy, 1790–1860: Sources and Readings* (New York: Harcourt, Brace & World, 1967), 80–81; Alan L. Olmstead and Paul W. Rhode, *Creating Abundance: Biological Innovation and American Agricultural Development* (Cambridge: Cambridge University Press, 2008), 100–114.

9. Beckert, *Empire of Cotton*, 105.

10. This story is related in detail in Adam Rothman, *Slave Country: American Expansion and the Origins of the Deep South* (Cambridge, MA: Harvard University Press, 2005); Lewis Cecil Gray, *History of Agriculture in the Southern United States to 1860*, 2 vols. (Washington, DC: Carnegie Institution of Washington, 1933), 2:709; John Hebron Moore, *The Emergence of the Cotton Kingdom in the Old South West, Mississippi, 1770–1860* (Baton Rouge: Louisiana State University Press, 1988), 6;

John F. Stover, *The Routledge Historical Atlas of the American Railroads* (New York: Routledge, 1999), 15.

11. The numbers are from Rothman, *Slave Country*, 11; John Craig Hammond, "Slavery, Settlement, and Empire: The Expansion and Growth of Slavery in the Interior of the North American Continent, 1770–1820," *Journal of Early Republic* 32 (Summer 2012): 175–206; Allan Kulikoff, "Uprooted People: Black Migrants in the Age of the American Revolution, 1790–1820," in *Slavery and Freedom in the Age of the American Revolution*, ed. Ira Berlin and Ronald Hoffmann (Charlottesville: University Press of Virginia, 1983), 149; Peter A. Coclanis and Lacy K. Ford, "The South Carolina Economy Reconstructed and Reconsidered: Structure, Output, and Performance, 1670–1985," in *Developing Dixie: Modernization in a Traditional Society*, ed. Winfred B. Moore Jr. (New York: Greenwood Press, 1988), 97; Kulikoff, "Uprooted People," 149.

12. *De Bow's Review* 11 (September 1851): 308; see also James Mann, *The Cotton Trade of Great Britain* (London: Simpkin, Marshall, 1860), 53; *American Cotton Planter* 1 (1853): 152; Beckert, *Empire of Cotton*, 108; Charles Mackenzie, *Facts, Relative to the Present State of the British Cotton Colonies and to the Connection of their Interests* (Edinburgh: James Clarke, 1811), 35; "Cotton Cultivation, Manufacture, and Foreign Trade of," letter from the secretary of the treasury, March 4, 1836 (Washington: Blair & Rives, 1836), 16, accessed July 29, 2013, http://catalog.hathitrust.org/Record/011159609.

13. Kulikoff, "Uprooted People," 143; James McMillan, "The Final Victims: The Demography, Atlantic Origins, Merchants, and Nature of the Post-Revolutionary Foreign Slave Trade to North America, 1783–1810" (PhD diss., Duke University, 1999), 40–98; Walter Johnson, introduction to *The Chattel Principle: Internal Slave Trades in the Americas*, ed. Walter Johnson (New Haven, CT: Yale University Press, 2004), 6; James A. B. Scherer, *Cotton as a World Power: A Study in the Economic Interpretation of History* (New York: F. A. Stokes, 1916), 151; Rothman, *Slave Country*, 182–188; Kulikoff, "Uprooted People," 149, 152; Michael Tadman, *Speculators and Slaves: Masters, Traders, and Slaves in the Old South* (Madison: University of Wisconsin Press, 1989), 12.

14. John H. Moore, "Two Cotton Kingdoms," *Agricultural History* 60 (Fall 1986): 1–16; Gavin Wright, *The Political Economy of the Cotton South: Households, Markets, and Wealth in the Nineteenth Century* (New York: W. W. Norton, 1978), 28; Ronald Bailey, "The Other Side of Slavery: Black Labor, Cotton, and Textile Industrialization in Great Britain and the United States," *Agricultural History* 68 (Spring 1994): 38; Wright, *Political Economy of the Cotton South*, 27.

15. At four hundred pounds to the bale. The numbers are from Moore, *Emergence of the Cotton Kingdom*, 129.

16. James C. Cobb, *The Most Southern Place on Earth: The Mississippi Delta and the Roots of Regional Identity* (New York: Oxford University Press, 1992), 8–10.

17. Bonnie Martin, "Slavery's Invisible Engine: Mortgaging Human Property," *Journal of Southern History* 76 (November 2010): 840–841.

18. C. Wayne Smith and J. Tom Cothren, eds., *Cotton: Origin, History, Technology, and Production* (New York: John Wiley & Sons, 1999), 103, 122. On the various origins of American cotton, see also Whitemarsh B. Seabrook, *A Memoir of the Origin, Cultivation and Uses of Cotton* (Charleston, SC: Miller & Browne, 1844), 15.

19. See, for this argument, Philip McMichael, "Slavery in Capitalism: The Rise and Demise of the U.S. Ante-Bellum Cotton Culture," *Theory and Society* 20 (June 1991): 335.

20. Ernst von Halle, *Baumwollproduktion und Pflanzungswirtschaft in den nordamerikanischen Süedstaaten*, part 1, *Die Sklavenzeit* (Leipzig: Verlag von Duncker & Humblot, 1897), viii; *Organization of the Cotton Power: Communication of the President* (Macon: Lewis B. Andrews Book and Job Printer, 1858), 7; *American Cotton Planter* 1 (January 1853): 11; Beckert, *Empire of Cotton*, 119.

21. See Sven Beckert, *The Monied Metropolis: New York City and the Consolidation of the American Bourgeoisie, 1850–1896* (Cambridge: Cambridge University Press, 2001).

22. August Etienne, *Die Baumwollzucht im Wirtschaftsprogram der deutschen Übersee-Politk* (Berlin: Verlag von Hermann Paetel, 1902), 28. Labor shortage was also an important subject in discussions on the expansion of Indian cotton production during the US Civil War. See for example *Times of India*, October 18, 1861, 3; February 27, 1863, 6; *Zeitfragen* (May 1, 1911): 1.

23. Kolonial-Wirtschaftliches Komitee, *Deutsch-koloniale Baumwoll-Unternehmungen, Bericht XI* (Spring 1909): 28, in 8224, R 1001, Bundesarchiv Berlin; Thaddeus Sunseri, "*Die Baumwollfrage*: Cotton Colonialism in German East Africa," *Central European History* 34 (2001): 46, 48. Peasant resistance against colonial cotton projects in a very different context is also described in Allen Isaacman et al., "'Cotton Is the Mother of Poverty': Peasant Resistance to Forced Cotton Production in Mozambique, 1938–1961," *International Journal of African Historical Studies* 13 (1980): 581–615; Kolonial-Wirtschaftliches Komitee, "Verhandlungen der Baumwoll-Kommission des Kolonial-Wirtschaftlichen Komitees vom 25. April 1912," 169; J. E. Horn, *La crise cotonnière et les textiles indigènes* (Paris: Dentu, 1863), 15; Timothy Mitchell, *Rule of Experts: Egypt, Techno-Politics and Modernity* (Berkeley: University of California Press, 2002), 59–60.

24. Mildred Gwin Andrews, *The Men and the Mills: A History of the Southern Textile Industry* (Macon, GA: Mercer University Press, 1987), 1; David L. Carlton and Peter A. Coclanis, "Southern Textiles in Global Context," in *Global Perspectives on Industrial Transformation in the American South*, ed. Susanna Delfino and Michele

Gillespie (Columbia: University of Missouri Press, 2005), 160; Alice Galenson, *The Migration of Cotton Textile Workers from New England to the South: 1880-1930* (New York: Garland, 1985), 2.

25. Elijah Helm, "An International of the Cotton Industry," *Quarterly Journal of Economics* 17 (May 1903): 428; Galenson, *Migration of Cotton Textile Workers*, 186; Melvin Thomas Copeland, *The Cotton Manufacturing Industry of the United States* (New York: A. M. Kelley, 1966), 46. See also Steven Hahn, *The Roots of Southern Populism: Yeoman Farmers and the Transformation of the Georgia Upcountry, 1850-1890* (New York: Oxford University Press, 1983); Copeland, *Cotton Manufacturing Industry*, 40; Gavin Wright, "The Economic Revolution in the American South," *Journal of Economic Perspectives* 1 (Summer 1987): 169. The story of how the transformation of Southern countryside is related to the emergence of wage workers in the American South is told by Barbara Fields, "The Nineteenth-Century American South: History and Theory," *Plantation Society in the Americas* 2 (April 1983): 7-27; Steven Hahn, "Class and State in Postemancipation Societies: Southern Planters in Comparative Perspective," *American Historical Review* 95 (February 1990): 75-88; *Southern and Western Textile Excelsior*, December 11, 1897, as cited in Beth English, "Capital Mobility and the 1890s U.S. Textile Industry," in *Global Perspectives on Industrial Transformation in the American South*, ed. Susanna Delfino and Michele Gillespie (Columbia: University of Missouri Press, 2005), 188.

26. Galenson, *Migration of Cotton Textile Workers*, 189-190; Carlton and Coclanis, "Southern Textiles in Global Context," 155, 156, 158; *Commercial Bulletin*, September 28, 1894, cited in Beth English, *A Common Thread: Labor, Politics, and Capital Mobility in the Textile Industry* (Athens: University of Georgia Press, 2006), 39; *Lynchburg News*, January 18, 1895, cited in English, "Capital Mobility and the 1890s U.S. Textile Industry," 176.

27. Galenson, *Migration of Cotton Textile Workers*, 141; Copeland, *Cotton Manufacturing Industry*, 42; Mary Blewett, "Textile Workers in the American Northeast and South: Shifting Landscapes of Class, Culture, Gender, Race, and Protest," paper presented at Global History of Textile Workers Conference / IISH, November 11-13, 2004, p. 12; See, for example, Katherine Rye Jewell, "Region and Subregion: Mapping Southern Economic Identity," unpublished paper presented at Social Science History Conference, Boston, November 17-20, 2011.

28. Brian Schoen, *The Fragile Fabric of Union: Cotton, Federal Politics and the Global Origins of the Civil War* (Baltimore: Johns Hopkins University Press, 2009), 157.

The Rise and Fall of American Sugar

1. Sidney Mintz, *Sweetness and Power: The Place of Sugar in Modern History* (New York: Viking Books, 1985), 41; Nöel Deerr, *The History of Sugar*, 2 vols. (Lon-

don: Chapman & Hall, 1949), 1:248; Philip Curtin, *The Rise and Fall of the Plantation Complex: Essays in Atlantic History* (Cambridge: Cambridge University Press, 1998); Stuart B. Schwartz, ed., *Tropical Babylons: Sugar and the Making of the Atlantic World, 1450–1680* (Chapel Hill: University of North Carolina Press, 2004); B. W. Higman, "The Sugar Revolution," *Economic History Review* 53 (May 2000): 213–236.

2. James Belich, *Replenishing The Earth: The Settler Revolution and the Rise of the Anglo-World, 1783–1939* (New York: Oxford University Press, 2009). Excellent overviews of nineteenth century sugar include J. H. Galloway, *The Sugar Cane Industry: An Historical Geography from Its Origins to 1914* (Cambridge: Cambridge University Press, 1989), 120–194; Bill Albert and Adrian Graves, eds., *Crisis and Change* in the *International Sugar Economy* (Edinburgh: ISC Press, 1984).

3. There is a wide literature on servitude, indenture, and the global search for sugar laborers; see Stanley L. Engerman, "Contract Labor, Sugar, and Technology in the Nineteenth Century," *Journal of Economic History* 53 (September 1983): 635–659; Sidney Mintz, "Slavery and the Rise of Peasantries," in *Roots and Branches: Current Directions in Slave Studies*, ed. Michael Craton (Toronto: Pergamon Press, 1979), 218–242; Rebecca J. Scott, "Defining the Boundaries of Freedom in the World of Cane: Cuba, Brazil, and Louisiana after Emancipation," *American Historical Review* 99 (February 1999): 70–102. On the enduring issue of planter power and patron-client relations as social determinants in plantation societies, see Arthur L. Stinchcombe, *Sugar Island Slavery in the Age of the Enlightenment: The Political Economy of the Caribbean World* (Princeton, NJ: Princeton University Press, 1995), 125–158; Steven Hahn, "Class and State in Postemancipation Societies: Southern Planters in Comparative Perspective," *American Historical Review* 95 (February 1990): 75–98; Pete Daniel, "The Metamorphosis of Slavery," *Journal of American History* 66 (June 1979): 88–89.

4. Sugar data from Deerr, *History of Sugar*, 1:112–113, 126, 131, 136, 141, 143, 191, 193–204, 224, 235–236, 240, 250–251, 258; William C. Stubbs, *Sugar Cane: A Treatise on the History, Botany, and Agriculture of Sugar Cane*, 2 vols. (Baton Rouge, LA: State Bureau of Agriculture and Immigration, 1897) 1:59–63; Nöel Deerr, *Cane Sugar* (London: Norman Rodgers, 1921), 29–35; Vincent A. Mahler, "Britain, the European Community, and the Developing Commonwealth: Dependence, Interdependence, and the Political Economy of Sugar," *International Organization* 35 (Summer 1981): 475; Lewis Sharpe Ware, *The Sugar Beet: Including a History of the Beet Sugar Industry in Europe, Varieties of the Sugar Beet . . .* (Philadelphia: H. C. Baird, 1880).

5. Galloway, *Sugar Cane Industry*, 121.

6. Robert Debs Heinl Jr. and Nancy Gordon Heinl, *Written in Blood: The Story of the Haitian People, 1492–1971* (Boston: Houghton Mifflin, 1978), 31 (quote); Charles Gayarré, *History of Louisiana*, 5 vols. (New Orleans: F. F. Hansell, 1903),

3:350 (quote); Shannon Lee Dawdy, *Building the Devil's Empire: French Colonial New Orleans* (Chicago: University of Chicago Press, 2008); Adam Rothman, *Slave Country: American Expansion and the Origins of the Deep South* (Cambridge, MA: Harvard University Press, 2005); Deerr, *History of Sugar*, 1:240; *De Bow's Review* 22 (June 1857): 618; Henry Rightor, *Standard History of New Orleans, Louisiana* (Chicago: Lewis, 1900), 650; René Le Gardeur Jr., "The Origins of the Sugar Industry in Louisiana," in *Greenfields: Two Hundred Years of Louisiana Sugar* (Lafayette: University of Southwestern Louisiana Press, 1980), 7–10.

7. Georges-Henri Victor Collot, *A Journey in North America, Containing a Survey of the Countries Watered by the Mississippi, Ohio, Missouri, and Other Affluing Rivers . . .* (repr., Florence: O. Lange, 1924), 93; James Pitot, *Observations on the Colony of Louisiana from 1796 to 1802*, trans. Henry C. Pitot (Baton Rouge: Louisiana State University, 1979), 74; Berquin Duvallon, *Travels in Louisiana and the Floridas in the Year 1802, Giving A Correct Picture of Those Countries*, trans John Davies (New York: I. Riley, 1806), 129; *An Account of Louisiana being an Abstract of Documents in the Offices of the Departments of State and of the Treasury* (Philadelphia: John Conrad, 1803), 32; John G. Clark, *New Orleans 1718–1812: An Economic History* (Baton Rouge: Louisiana State University Press, 1970), 219. An arpent was a French land measurement that varied but typically measured .84 acres. Craig A. Bauer, *Creole Genesis: The Bringier Family and Antebellum Plantation Life in Louisiana* (Lafayette: University of Louisiana at Lafayette Press, 2011), 150.

8. W. C. C. Claiborne to Thomas Jefferson, July 10, 1806, in *Official Letter Books of W. C. C. Claiborne, 1801–1816*, ed. Dunbar Rowland, 6 vols. (Jackson, MS: State Department of Archives and History, 1917), 3:363; Henry Marie Brackenridge, *Views of Louisiana: Together With a Journal Up the Missouri River in 1811* (repr., Chicago: Quadrangle Books, 1962), 175; Samuel Hambleton to David Porter, January 25, 1811, David Dixon Porter Family Papers, Manuscript Division, Library of Congress, Washington, DC. The best historical overview on the 1811 revolt to date is Robert Paquette, "'A Horde of Brigands'? The Great Louisiana Slave Revolt of 1811 Reconsidered," *Historical Reflections* 35 (Spring 2009), 72–96; *Historical Census Browser*. Retrieved September 30, 2013, from the University of Virginia, Geospatial and Statistical Data Center, http://mapserver.lib.virginia.edu/.

9. Pierre C. de Laussat, *Mémoire sur ma vie pendant les années 1802 et suivantes* (Pau, France: Vignancour, 1831), 164; F. D. Richardson, "The Teche Country Fifty Years Ago," *Southern Bivouac* 4 (March 1886): 593; *Planters' Banner* (Franklin, LA), March 15, 1848; William Darby, *The Emigrants Guide to the Western and Southwestern States and Territories* (New York: Kirk & Mercein, 1818), 75. On prices, Arthur Harrison Cole, *Wholesale Commodity Prices in the United States, 1700–1861: Statistical Supplement Actual Wholesale Prices of Various Commodities* (Cambridge, MA: Harvard University Press, 1938), 175–275.

10. *De Bow's Review* 1 (January 1846): 55–56; Richard Follett, *The Sugar Masters: Planters and Slaves in Louisiana's Cane World, 1820–1860* (Baton Rouge: Louisiana State University, 2005), 48–54; US Bureau of the Census, *Third, Fourth, Fifth Census of the United States* (Washington, DC: 1811–1831).

11. *Hunt's Merchant Magazine* 39 (November 1858): 550; *Farmer's Cabinet and American Herd Book* 2 (October 1837): 78; *Journal of Agriculture* 1 (December 1845): 281; *Hunt's Merchant Magazine* 27 (December 1852): 679; Robert Fogel, *Without Consent or Contract: The Rise and Fall of American Slavery* (New York: W. W. Norton, 1989), 85; Robert A. Margo and Georgia C. Villaflor, "Growth of Wages in Antebellum America: New Evidence," *Journal of Economic History* 47 (December 1987): 873–895; Robert A. Margo, "Wages and Prices during the Antebellum Period: A Survey and New Evidence," in *American Economic Growth and Standards of Living before the Civil War*, ed. Robert E. Gallman and John J. Wallis (Chicago: University of Chicago Press, 1992), 183. On sugar prices, see *Historical Statistics of the United States: Colonial Times to 1957* (Washington, DC: Government Printing Office, 1960), 124.

12. *De Bow's Review* 4 (April 1848): 367; *Monthly Journal of Agriculture* 1 (March 1846): 462–463; E. Merton Coulter, *Thomas Spalding of Sapelo* (Baton Rouge: Louisiana State University Press, 1940); J. Carlyle Sitterson, "Ante-Bellum Sugar Culture in the South Atlantic States," *Journal of Southern History* 3 (May 1937): 175–187.

13. On cane farming, W. J. Evans, *The Sugar Planter's Manual, Being a Treatise on the Art of Obtaining Sugar from the Sugar-Cane* (Philadelphia: Lea and Blanchard, 1848); Sam B. Hilliard, "Site Characteristics of the Louisiana Sugar Cane Industry," *Agricultural History* 53 (January 1979): 254–269; John B. Rehder, *Delta Sugar: Louisiana's Vanishing Landscape* (Baltimore: Johns Hopkins University Press, 1999); *New Orleans Price Current*, September 1, 1847, reprinted in *Hunt's Merchant Magazine* 19 (November 1848): 490–491.

14. *American Agriculturist* 9 (November 1850): 351; *De Bow's Review* 1 (January 1846): 55; *Hunt's Merchant Magazine* 30 (May 1854): 499; P. A. Champomier, *Statement of the Sugar Crop Made in Louisiana in 1853–1854* (New Orleans: Cook, Young, 1854), 42; Champomier, *Statement of Sugar Crop in 1859–60*, 39; Richard Follett, "Old South, New South: The Strange Career of Pierre Champomier," in *The Enigmatic South: Toward Civil War and Its Legacies*, ed. Samuel C. Hyde Jr. (Baton Rouge: Louisiana State University Press, 2015), 153–173; J. Carlyle Sitterson, *Sugar Country: The Cane Sugar Industry in the South, 1753–1950* (Lexington: University of Kentucky Press, 1953), 177; Karl Joseph Menn, *The Large Slaveholders of Louisiana—1860* (New Orleans: Pelican, 1964), 6–31.

15. *De Bow's Review* 1 (January 1846): 55–56; *Hunt's Merchants' Magazine* 30 (April 1854): 499; Menn, *Large Slaveholders of Louisiana*, 23. On slave importation to the sugar region, see Follett, *Sugar Masters*, 48–69; Michael Tadman, "The De-

mographic Cost of Sugar: Debates on Societies and Natural Increase in the Americas," *American Historical Review* 105 (December 2000): 1570–1573.

16. Richard Follett, "Slavery and Technology in Louisiana's Sugar Bowl," in *Technology, Innovation and Southern Industrialization: From the Antebellum Era to the Computer Age*, ed. Susanna Delfino and Michele Gillespie (Columbia: University of Missouri Press, 2008), 68–96. On the transformation from horse to steam power, see *De Bow's Review* 1 (January 1846): 55; Charles L. Fleischmann, "Report on Sugar Cane and Its Culture," US Patent Office, *Annual Report of the Commissioner of Patents for the Year 1848*, 30th Cong., 2nd sess., House of Representatives Doc. No. 59 (Washington, DC: Wendell and Van Benthuysen, 1849), 294; *Planters' Banner* (Franklin), July 29, 1847; Edward J. Forstall, *Agricultural Productions of Louisiana, Embracing Valuable Information Relative to the Cotton, Sugar and Molasses Interests, and the Effects upon the Same of the Tariff of 1842* (New Orleans: Tropic Print, 1845), 4; J. A. Leon, *On Sugar Cultivation in Louisiana, Cuba, etc., and the British Possessions by a European and Colonial Sugar Manufacturer* (London: J. Ollivier, 1848), 26; Champomier, *Statement of Sugar Crop in 1850–51*, 43; *Statement of Sugar Crop in 1860–1861*, 39; J. S. Johnston, *Letter of Mr. Johnston of Louisiana to the Secretary of Treasury . . . relative to the Culture of the Sugar Cane* (Washington, DC: Gales and Seaton, 1831), 8; *De Bow's Review* (November 1847): 385–386.

17. Richard Follett, *Documenting Louisiana Sugar, 1844–1917*, 2008, www.sussex.ac.uk/louisianasugar; James D. B. De Bow, *The Industrial Resources etc., of the Southern and Western States*, 3 vols. (New Orleans: Office of De Bow's Review, 1853), 2:206; *De Bow's Review* 4 (1847): 425. On antebellum technology and slavery, see Follett, *Sugar Masters*, 90–150; Sitterson, *Sugar Country*, 112–156; John Heitmann, *Modernization of the Louisiana Sugar Industry, 1830–1910* (Baton Rouge: Louisiana State University Press, 1987), 1–48; Mark Schmitz, "Economies of Scale and Farm Size in the Antebellum Sugar Sector," *Journal of Economic History* 37 (December 1977): 959–980.

18. James Ramsay, *An Essay on the Treatment and Conversion of African Slaves in the British Sugar Colonies* (London: James Phillips, 1784), 69; Follett, *Sugar Masters*, 46–117.

19. Dale Tomich, *Through the Prism of Slavery: Labor, Control, and World Economy* (Lanham, MD: Rowman and Littlefield, 2004), 56–71; Anthony Kaye, "The Second Slavery: Modernity in the Nineteenth-Century South and the Atlantic World," *Journal of Southern History* 75 (August 2009): 627–650; Edward E. Baptist, *The Half Has Never Been Told: Slavery and the Making of American Capitalism* (New York: Basic Books, 2014), 128.

20. On Caribbean competition (especially in New York), DeBow, *Industrial Resources*, 2:312; P. A. Champomier, *Statement of Sugar Crop in 1851–1852*, 49; *Statement of Sugar Crop in 1857–1858*, 41–42; *Statement of Sugar Crop in 1860–1861*, 41–42.

21. W. H. Stephenson, *Alexander Porter: Whig Planter of Old Louisiana* (Baton Rouge: Louisiana State University Press, 1934), 27.

22. *Sugar Planter* (Port Allen, LA), April 3, 1869; Richard Follett, Eric Foner, and Walter Johnson, *Slavery's Ghost: The Problem of Freedom in the Age of Emancipation* (Baltimore: Johns Hopkins University Press, 2011), 56–70; John C. Rodrigue, *Reconstruction in the Cane Fields: From Slavery to Free Labor in Louisiana's Sugar Parishes, 1862–1880* (Baton Rouge: Louisiana State University, 2001), 120–138; Thomas C. Holt, *The Problem of Freedom: Race, Labor, and Politics in Jamaica and Britain* (Baltimore: Johns Hopkins University Press, 1992), 143.

23. *Louisiana Sugar Bowl* (Lafayette), July 15, 1880; Richard Follett and Rick Halpern, "From Slavery to Freedom in Louisiana's Sugar Country: Changing Labor Systems and Workers' Power, 1861–1913," in *Sugar, Slavery, and Society: Perspectives on the Caribbean, India, the Mascarenes, and the United States*, ed. Bernard Moitt (Gainesville: University Press of Florida, 2004), 135–156; Moon Ho-Jung, *Coolies and Cane: Race, Labor, and Sugar in the Age of Emancipation* (Baltimore: Johns Hopkins University Press, 2006), 73–106. Laird W. Bergad, *Cuban Rural Society in the Nineteenth Century: The Social and Economic History of Monoculture in Matanzas* (Princeton, NJ: Princeton University Press, 1990), 249; Madhavi Kale, *Fragments of Empire: Capital, Slavery, and Indian Indentured Labor Migration in the British Caribbean* (Philadelphia: University of Pennsylvania Press, 1998); Peter L. Eisenberg, *The Sugar Industry in Pernambuco: Modernization without Change* (Los Angeles: University of California Press, 1974), 198–214; Harmannus Hoetink, "Labour 'Scarcity' and Immigration in the Dominican Republic c. 1875–c. 1930," in *Labour in the Caribbean*, ed. Malcolm Cross and Gad Heuman (London: Macmillan, 1988), 160–175.

24. Richard J. Amundson, "Oakley Plantation: A Post-Civil War Venture in Louisiana Sugar," *Louisiana History* 9 (Winter 1968): 31; Mary Pugh to Edward F. Pugh, November 25, 1997, Mary W. Pugh Papers, Louisiana and Lower Mississippi Valley Collections, Hill Memorial Library, Louisiana State University, Baton Rouge, LA; Rebecca J. Scott, *Degrees of Freedom: Louisiana and Cuba after Slavery* (Cambridge, MA: Harvard University Press, 2005), 77–93; James K. Hogue, *Uncivil War: Five New Orleans Street Battles and the Rise and Fall of Radical Reconstruction* (Baton Rouge: Louisiana State University Press, 2006), 180–194.

25. Rick Halpern, "Solving the 'Labour Problem': Race, Work, and the State in the Sugar Industries of Louisiana and Natal, 1870–1910," *Journal of Southern African Studies* 30 (March 2004): 19–40; Demetrius L. Eudell, *The Political Languages of Emancipation in the British Caribbean and the U.S. South* (Chapel Hill: University of North Carolina Press, 2002), 43–65; Matthew Pratt Guterl, *American Mediterranean: Southern Slaveholders in the Age of Emancipation* (Cambridge, MA: Harvard University Press, 2008), 114–146.

26. Mark Schmitz, "The Transformation of the Southern Cane Sugar Sector, 1860–1930," *Agricultural History* 53 (January 1979): 271; Sitterson, *Sugar Country*, 296; Louis Ferleger, "Cutting the Cane: Harvesting in the Louisiana Sugar Industry," *Southern Studies* 23 (Spring 1984): 42–59; Louis Ferleger, "Farm Mechanization in the Southern Sugar Sector after the Civil War," *Louisiana History* 23 (Winter 1982): 21–34; Jean Ann Scarpaci, "Immigrants in the New South: Italians in Louisiana's Sugar Parishes, 1880–1910," *Labor History* 16 (Spring 1975): 165–183; Scott, "Defining the Boundaries," 78.

27. César J. Ayala, *American Sugar Kingdom: The Plantation Economy of the Spanish Caribbean, 1898–1934* (Chapel Hill: University of North Carolina Press, 1999), 30, 66–67; Wendy A. Woloson, *Refined Tastes: Sugar, Confectionary, and Consumers in Nineteenth-Century America* (Baltimore: Johns Hopkins University Press, 2002), 187.

28. Deerr, *History of Sugar*, 1:112–113, 126, 131, 136, 143, 204, 224, 250, 258; 2:490–491.

29. Ibid., 2:492–498.

30. Alfred S. Eichner, *The Emergence of Oligopoly: Sugar Refining as a Case Study* (Baltimore: Johns Hopkins University Press, 1969), 78–82; Thomas Becnel, *Labor, Church, and Sugar Establishment: Louisiana, 1887–1976* (Baton Rouge: Louisiana State University Press, 1980), 71–72; Paul S. Vogt, *The Sugar Refining Industry of the United States: Its Development and Present Condition* (Philadelphia: Publications of the University of Pennsylvania, 1908). The reciprocity treaties offered producers in Cuba a 20 percent reduction on the tariff on raw sugar.

31. Richard Sheridan, "Changing Sugar Technology and the Labour Nexus in the British Caribbean, 1750–1900 with Special Reference to Barbados and Jamaica," *New West India Guide* 63 (1989): 60–92; Howard Temperley, ed., *After Slavery: Emancipation and Its Discontents* (London: Frank Cass, 2000), 196; Jonathan Curry-Machado, *Cuban Sugar Industry: Transnational Migrants and Engineering Migrants in Mid-nineteenth Century Cuba* (London: Palgrave, 2011); Francisco A. Scarano, *Sugar and Slavery in Puerto Rico: The Plantation Economy of Ponce, 1800–1850* (Madison: University of Wisconsin Press, 1984), 100–119; Alan Dye, *Cuban Sugar in the Age of Mass Production: Technology and the Economics of the Sugar Central, 1899–1929* (Stanford, CA: Stanford University Press, 1998), 66–149.

32. Ayala, *American Sugar Kingdom*, 23–120, 188–189; Ralph Shlomowitz, "Plantations and Smallholdings: Comparative Perspectives from the World Cotton and Sugar Cane Economies," *Agricultural History* 59 (July 1984): 1–16; John A. Heitmann, "Responding to the Competition: The Louisiana Sugar Planters Association, the Tariff, and the Formation of the Louisiana Sugar Exchange, 1877–1885," *Southern Studies* 25 (Winter 1986): 315–340. As an example of increased yields, note the aggregate production of Central Francisco (Camagüey, Cuba) in 1902: 1,651

tons; 1910: 19,814 tons; 1918: (during the height of WWI sugar fever) 51,724 tons. Ayala, *Sugar Kingdom*, 131.

33. *The Machinery and Equipment of the Louisiana Cane Sugar Factories* (New Orleans: A. B. Gilmore, 1923), 48–49; US Department of Commerce, *The Sugar Industry*, Bureau of Foreign and Domestic Commerce, Miscellaneous Series 9 (Washington, DC: Government Printing Office, 1913), 61–62; Alcee Bouchereau, *Statement of the Sugar and Rice Crops Made in Louisiana in 1879–80 and 1899–1900* (New Orleans: Young, Bright, 1869–1901); Schmitz, "Transformation of the Southern Cane Sugar Sector," 274; Deerr, *History of Sugar*, 2:556–577.

34. Michael G. Wade, *Sugar Dynasty: M. A. Patout & Son, Ltd, 1791–1993* (Lafayette: University of Southwestern Louisiana Press, 1995), 168–185; Sitterson, *Sugar Country*, 307; Schmitz, "Transformation of the Southern Cane Sugar Sector," 277.

35. Speech of William C. Stubbs (undated) to Ways and Means Committee, William C. Stubbs Papers, Southern Historical Collection, Wilson Library, University of North Carolina, Chapel Hill; Heitmann, *Modernization*, 169–243; Deerr, *History of Sugar*, 2:586–597.

36. Sitterson, *Sugar Country*, 266, 348; Gail M. Hollander, *Raising Cane in the 'Glades: The Global Sugar Trade and the Transformation of Florida* (Gainesville: University Press of Florida, 2008).

Tobacco's Commodity Route

1. Lewis Cecil Gray, *History of Agriculture in the Southern United States to 1860*, 2 vols. (Washington, DC: Carnegie Institution of Washington, 1933), 1:218; "Type-Classification of American-Grown Tobacco," USDA Miscellaneous Circular No. 55 (Washington, DC: US Government Printing Office, 1925).

2. W. W. Garner, "Some Observations on Tobacco Breeding," *Proceedings of the Meeting of the American Breeders Association*, 8 (January 1912): 460–462; W. W. Garner, H. A. Allard, and E. E. Clayton, "Superior Germ Plasm in Tobacco," in USDA *Yearbook* 1936 (Washington, DC: US Government Printing Office, 1937), 819; B. C. Yang et al., "Assessing the Genetic Diversity of Tobacco Germplasm," *Annals of Applied Biology* 150 (published online June 5, 2007): 393; Alan L. Olmstead and Paul W. Rhode, "The Red Queen and the Hard Reds: Productivity Growth in American Wheat, 1800–1940," *Journal of Economic History* 62 (December 2002): 929–966, esp. 931n7; Amy B. Trubek, *The Taste of Place: A Cultural Journey into Terroir* (Berkeley: University of California Press, 2008). Before the twentieth century and its establishment of the gene as a unit of inheritable characteristics, the scientists of heritability were as interested in flow and change and evolution as in discrete units of heritable material. None assumed that a varietal was a stable product of the seed. See "Appendix: The Real Thing; Tobacco Genetics," in *Making Tobacco*

Bright: Creating an American Commodity, 1617–1937, by Barbara Hahn (Baltimore: Johns Hopkins University Press, 2011).

3. Thomas W. Crowder to William Gray, October 18, 1846, William Gray Papers, Virginia Historical Society, Richmond, VA; Robert A. Martin to Wm. Henry Burwell, July 23, 1872, Folder 44, Box 2, Series 1.2; Martin Hill & Co to Wm. H. Burwell, October 25, 1879, Folder 49, Box 2, Series 1.2, both, Burwell Family Papers, Southern Historical Collection, University of North Carolina, Chapel Hill, NC.

4. Hahn, *Making Tobacco Bright.*

5. Edmund S. Morgan, "The Labor Problem at Jamestown, 1607–18," *American Historical Review* 76 (June 1971): 595–611; Russell R. Menard, "The Tobacco Industry in the Chesapeake Colonies, 1617–1730," *Research in Economic History* 5 (1980): 109–177; John Elliot, *Empires of the Atlantic World: Britain and Spain in America, 1492–1830* (New Haven, CT: Yale University Press, 2006); John J. McCusker and Russell R. Menard, *The Economy of British America, 1607–1789* (Chapel Hill: University of North Carolina Press, 1985; repr. ed., 1991), 118; Hahn, *Making Tobacco Bright*, 38–40.

6. Virginia General Assembly, *Journals of the House of Burgesses* (Richmond: Virginia State Library, 1905–1915), 1:17, 47, 53.

7. Allan Kulikoff, *Tobacco and Slaves: The Development of Southern Cultures in the Chesapeake, 1680–1800* (Chapel Hill: University of North Carolina Press, 1986), 107–112, 112 (quote); *A Dialogue Between Thomas Sweet-Scented, William Oronoco . . .* , pamphlet, 3rd ed., 1732, p. 10; Charles E. Gage, *Tobacco, Tobacco Hogsheads, and Rolling Roads*, paper read before the Falls Church Historical Commission, July 18, 1959, p. 4.

8. Frederick F. Siegel, *Roots of Southern Distinctiveness* (Chapel Hill: University of North Carolina Press, 1987), 62.

9. Lois Green Carr and Russell R. Menard, "Land, Labor, and Economies of Scale in Early Maryland," *Journal of Economic History* 49 (June 1989): 407, 413; Hahn, *Making Tobacco Bright*, 44, 122, 164.

10. For an introduction to the interactions between race and slavery in the colonial Chesapeake, see Edmund S. Morgan, *American Slavery, American Freedom: The Ordeal of Colonial Virginia* (New York: W. W. Norton, 1975); Kathleen M. Brown, *Good Wives, Nasty Wenches, Anxious Patriarchs: Gender, Race, and Power in Colonial Virginia* (Chapel Hill: University of North Carolina Press, 1996). For a good introduction to science and technology studies, see John M. Staudenmaier, SJ, introduction to *Technology's Storytellers: Reweaving the Human Fabric* (Cambridge, MA: MIT Press, 1985); Staudenmaier, "The Society and Its Journal: The Emergence of Shared Discourse," in *Technology's Storytellers*, chapter 1; John K. [Jack] Brown, "Louis C. Hunter's *Steamboats on the Western Rivers*," *Technology and Culture* 44 (October 2003): 786–793; Langdon Winner, "Do Artifacts Have Poli-

tics?," in *The Whale and the Reactor: A Search for Limits in the Age of High Technology* (Chicago: University of Chicago Press, 1986): 19–39; and Gabrielle Hecht, "Technopolitical Regimes," in *The Radiance of France: Nuclear Power and National Identity after World War II* (Cambridge, MA: MIT Press, 1998): 55–90. For a concise and useful treatment of the black box, see Bruno Latour, "Opening Pandora's Black Box," in *Science in Action: How to Follow Engineers and Scientists through Society* (Cambridge, MA: Harvard University Press, 1987), 1–16.

11. Jordan Paper, *Offering Smoke: The Sacred Pipe and Native American Religion* (Moscow: University of Idaho Press, 1988); R. Douglas Hurt, *Indian Agriculture in America: Prehistory to the Present* (Lawrence: University Press of Kansas, 1987), 45–48, 61.

12. Gray, *History of Agriculture*, 1:69–73, 1:70 (quote); "The Cultivation of Tobacco," *De Bow's Review* 9 (August 1855): 241–242.

13. George J. F. Clarke, "On Spanish Tobacco, &c.," *Southern Agriculturalist* 1 (June 1828): 259; W. H. Simmons, "On the Cultivation of Cuba Tobacco, by Joseph M. Hernandez," *Southern Agriculturalist* 3 (September 1830): 458–467.

14. William Tatham, *An Historical and Practical Essay on the Culture and Commerce of Tobacco* (London: Vernor and Hood, 1800; repr. ed., Miami, FL: University of Miami Press, 1969); James Jennings, *A Practical Treatise on the History, Medical Properties, and Cultivation of Tobacco* (London: Sherwood, Gilbert and Piper, 1830), 40.

15. Hahn, *Making Tobacco Bright*, 36. The term *peak labor demand* can be found in Howard Bodenhorn, "A Troublesome Caste: Height and Nutrition of Antebellum Virginia's Rural Free Blacks," *Journal of Economic History* 59 (December 1999): 978. The ways fixed investments in slaves required year-round employment is known as Genovese's law; see Eugene D. Genovese, "The Medical and Insurance Costs of Slaveholding in the Cotton Belt," *Journal of Negro History* 45 (July 1960): 141–155; and Ralph V. Anderson and Robert E. Gallman, "Slaves as Fixed Capital: Slave Labor and Southern Economic Development," *Journal of American History* 64 (June 1977): 24–46.

16. Carr and Menard, *Land, Labor, and Economies of Scale*, 410; Lorena S. Walsh, *Motives of Honor, Pleasure and Profit: Plantation Management in the Colonial Chesapeake, 1607–1763* (Chapel Hill: University of North Carolina Press, 2010), 524–538.

17. Peter A. Coclanis, *The Shadow of a Dream: Economic Life and Death in the South Carolina Low Country, 1670–1920* (New York: Oxford University Press, 1989), 194–195n15; McCusker and Menard, *Economy of British America*, chapter 2.

18. McCusker and Menard, *Economy of British America*, 124; Jacob M. Price, *Capital and Credit in British Overseas Trade* (Cambridge, MA: Harvard University Press, 1980), 96–97; Thomas Martin Devine, *Tobacco Lords: A Study of the Merchants of Glasgow and Their Trading Activities, ca. 1740–1790* (Edinburgh: Edinburgh University Press, 1990; orig. pub. 1975).

19. J. & D. Walker to Chris Winfree, April 19, 1845, Folder 7, Box 1, William E. Uzzell Papers, Southern Historical Collection; on curing methods, see Joseph C. Robert, *Tobacco Kingdom: Plantation, Market and Factory in Virginia and North Carolina, 1800–1860* (Durham, NC: Duke University Press, 1938), 38–46.

20. Ramon de Cozar to Charles Palmer, September 9, 1835, Palmer Family Papers, Virginia Historical Society; James Gray, March 23, 1842 (or his letter to the Richmond Whig, December 18, 1840), in Secretary of the Treasury, "Tobacco," May 28, 1842, H.R. doc. 235 (27-2) 404, pp. 85–86.

21. Treasury, "Tobacco," 19, 48; according to my calculations on the data in this source, the average annual figures between 1824 and 1833 were 19,077,716 pounds imported for Britons' internal consumption and 14,238,551 pounds imported for re-exportation elsewhere.

22. "Sales Eight Hogsheads Tobacco by Deane & Brown," account sales, September 23, 1854, Allen Family Papers, Virginia Historical Society; Samuel Nowlin to Dickenson, Pannill & Co., May 27, 1828, Folder 2, Box 1, Robert Wilson Papers, Southern Historical Collection.

23. A. Petricolas & Co. to Messrs. Peters & Whitehead, September 16, 1830, Folder 1, Box 1, Floyd L. Whitehead Papers, Southern Historical Collection; Thomas Branch & Bro. to Brooking Elder, May 29, 1846, Letterbook, May 10, 1846–August 16, 1849, Thomas Branch & Co. Papers, Virginia Historical Society.

24. Henry Fitzhugh to James Russell, ca. November 29, 1760 (letter not sent, crossed out); Henry Fitzhugh to James Buchanan, June 7, 1748; both, Letterbook 1746–1774, Henry Fitzhugh Papers, Perkins Library Special Collections, Duke University, Durham, NC; J. B. Killebrew, "Report on the Culture and Curing of Tobacco in the United States," in *Report on the Productions of Agriculture as Returned at the Tenth Census*, 3 vols. (Washington, DC: US Government Printing Office, 1883), 3:815; Jack P. Greene, ed., *Diary of Colonel Landon Carter* (Charlottesville: University Press of Virginia, 1965), 1:84, s.v. March 13, 1752; Victor S. Clark, *History of Manufactures in the United States, 1607–1860* (Washington, DC: Carnegie Institution, 1916), 18–19; Jacob M. Price, "The Beginnings of Tobacco Manufacture in Virginia," *Virginia Magazine of History and Biography* 64 (January 1956): 3–29.

25. Kennett, Dudley, & Co. to W. T. Sutherlin, January 10, 1860, Folder 4, Box 1, William T. Sutherlin Papers, Southern Historical Collection; Hahn, *Making Tobacco Bright*, chapter 2.

26. Hahn, *Making Tobacco Bright*, 42; Leland Smith, "A History of the Tobacco Industry in Kentucky from 1763 to 1860" (master's thesis, University of Kentucky, 1950).

27. On Spanish hunger for the goods of Kentucky settlers, see materials in the Pontalba Papers, Wilkinson-Miro Correspondence; Wilkinson's Memorial in the Temple Bodley Collection; all, translated and transcribed by Gilbert Pemberton

in the 1910s from the Louisiana Historical Society, New Orleans, now lodged in the Filson Historical Society, Louisville, KY. The originals were destroyed in France during the First World War. Many thanks to Kathleen DuVal for providing me with these materials. For the persistence of the Kentucky trade through New Orleans in the nineteenth century, see "The Tobacco Trade," *De Bow's Review* 2 (July 1846): 42–46; "New Tobacco Inspection Laws," *De Bow's Review* 2 (November 1846): 355–360.

28. Treasury, "Tobacco," p. 5; Gray, *History of Agriculture*, 1:443; Hahn, *Making Tobacco Bright*, table 2.1, p. 48.

29. Robert B. Campbell to R. M. T. Hunter, March 16, 1855, written on Horatio N. Davis, "Tobacco," price-circular, Mar. 1, 1855, Correspondence, Robert Mercer Taliaferro Hunter Papers, Virginia Historical Society; "Tobacco Trade with Europe, July 25, 1848," H.R. Rep. No 810 (30-1) 527; S. Doc. No. 55 (27-1) 390.

30. no. & Wm. Oxley to Towles and Soaper, June 30, 1840, Folder 15; Evans and Trokes to Towles and Soaper, circular letter, July 4, 1842, Folder 19; both, Towles and Soaper Papers, Filson Historical Society; Evans and Trokes to Towles and Soaper, circular letter, April 3, 1843, Folder 20, Towles and Soaper Papers, Filson Historical Society; Alexr. B. Barret to David Bullock Harris, February 10, 1843, Folder Correspondence/Papers 1843, January–May, David Bullock Harris Papers, Perkins Library Special Collections.

31. Hahn, *Making Tobacco Bright*, 76–77, and table 3.1; A. Hunter Dupree, *Science in the Federal Government: A History of Policies and Activities to 1940* (Cambridge, MA: Harvard University Press, 1957); Alan I. Marcus, *Agricultural Science and the Quest for Legitimacy: Farmers, Agricultural Colleges, and Experiment Stations, 1870–1890* (Ames: Iowa State University Press, 1985).

32. Hahn, *Making Tobacco Bright*, 101–107, 157–158, 164–166; Richard Franklin Bensel, *Yankee Leviathan: The Origins of Central State Authority in America, 1859–1877* (Cambridge: Cambridge University Press, 1991).

33. Alfred D. Chandler Jr., *The Visible Hand: The Managerial Revolution in American Business* (Cambridge, MA: Harvard University Press, 1977), 249–250, 290–291, 382, 388; Walter Licht, *Industrializing America: The Nineteenth Century* (Baltimore: Johns Hopkins University Press, 1995), 127, 145; Naomi R. Lamoreaux, *The Great Merger Movement in American Business, 1895–1940* (Cambridge: Cambridge University Press, 1985), 3, table 1.2; Leslie Hannah, "The Whig Fable of American Tobacco," *Journal of Economic History* 66 (March 2006): 64; Hahn, *Making Tobacco Bright*, 91–97.

34. Angela Lakwete, *Inventing the Cotton Gin: Machine and Myth in Antebellum America* (Baltimore: Johns Hopkins University Press, 2003), 55; Sean Price, *Smokestacks and Spinning Jennys: Industrial Revolution* (London: Heineman-Raintree, 2006), 6.

35. For an accessible explanation of the "plantation illusion" or "plantation ideal," see Everett Carter, "Cultural History Written with Lightning: The Significance of *The Birth of a Nation* (1915)," in *Hollywood as Historian: American Film in a Cultural Context*, ed. Peter C. Rollins (Lexington: University Press of Kentucky, 1983), 9–19.

36. Tobacco Institute, *Kentucky's Tobacco Heritage*, pamphlet, Folder 333, Box 4, Series 4.4, Universal Leaf Tobacco Company Papers, Virginia Historical Society; Killebrew, "Report on the Culture and Curing of Tobacco," in *Tenth Census*, 3:668–670.

37. Treasury, "Tobacco," 5; Killebrew, "Report on the Culture and Curing of Tobacco," in *Tenth Census*, 3:668, 674.

38. Alexr. B. Barret to David Bullock Harris, Feb. 10, 1843; Killebrew, "Report on the Culture and Curing of Tobacco," in *Tenth Census*, 3:652.

39. Christopher Waldrep, *Night Riders: Defending Community in the Black Patch, 1880–1915* (Durham, NC: Duke University Press, 1993), 79, 87–89, 95–98, 146–160; Tracy Campbell, *The Politics of Despair: Power and Resistance in the Tobacco Wars* (Lexington: University Press of Kentucky, 1993), 46, 48–51, 72, 78–81, 89–92; Elliot Jaspin, *Buried in the Bitter Waters: The Hidden History of Racial Cleansing in America* (New York: Basic Books, 2007), 87–107.

40. "Negroes Shot and Whipped," *Louisville Courier-Journal*, March 11, 1908, quoted in Jaspin, *Buried in the Bitter Waters*, 95–100, 99 (quote); Robert Penn Warren, *Night Rider* (New York: Random House, 1939), 260, 305–306; Campbell, *Politics of Despair*, 77–93; C. Vann Woodward, *Origins of the New South* (Baton Rouge: Louisiana State University Press, 1951), 327; James Michael Rhyne, "Rehearsal for Redemption: The Politics of Post-Emancipation Violence in Kentucky's Bluegrass Region" (PhD diss., University of Cincinnati, 2006), 190–193, 249–251.

41. "Free Tobacco Bill," March 1, 1907, S. Doc. No. 372 (59-2) 5073, pp. 35, 38; W. W. Garner et al., "History and Status of Tobacco Culture," in USDA *Yearbook* 1922 (Washington, DC: US Government Printing Office, 1923), 427, fig. 19; Genovese, "Medical and Insurance Costs of Slaveholding"; Anderson and Gallman, "Slaves as Fixed Capital"; Killebrew, "Report on the Culture and Curing," in *Tenth Census*, 3:653.

42. "That's All," *Hopkinsville Kentuckian*, May 22, 1896, p. 22. Thanks to Bruce E. Baker for bringing this source to my attention. J. P. Thompson & Co., "First Relief for Oppressed Black Patch Farmers," advertisement, *Hopkinsville Kentuckian*, April 3, 1909, sec. 2, p. 12; Bill Cunningham, *On Bended Knees: The Night Rider Story* (Nashville, TN: McClanahan, 1983), 53; "Tobacco Schedules 1910," Entry 309, Record Group 29, National Archives and Records Administration, Washington, DC.

43. Barbara Hahn, "Paradox of Precision: Bright Tobacco as Technology Transfer, 1880–1937," *Agricultural History* 82 (Spring 2008): 220–235.

44. Killebrew, "Report on the Culture and Curing," in *Tenth Census*, 3:704–705. For burley as bright, see J. B. Killebrew and Herbert Myrick, *Tobacco Leaf: Its Culture and Cure, Marketing and Manufacture* (New York: Orange Judd, 1897; repr. ed., 1934), 339.

45. J. H. Owen to William Thomas Sutherlin, September 20, 1861, Folder 13, Box 2; Hill & Warren to Samuel Ayres & Son, January 14, 1862, Folder 15, Box 2; Hill & Warren to Sutherlin, January 20, 1862, Folder 15, Box 2; all, William T. Sutherlin Papers, Southern Historical Collection.

46. Nannie May Tilley, *The Bright-Tobacco Industry* (Chapel Hill: University of North Carolina Press, 1948), 24; Killebrew, "Report on the Culture and Curing," in *Tenth Census*, 3:704; M. Ruth Little, *An Inventory of Historic Architecture, Caswell County, North Carolina* (Raleigh: North Carolina Department of Cultural Resources, 1979), 162; Eldred E. Prince Jr. with Robert A. Simpson, *Long Green: The Rise and Fall of Tobacco in South Carolina* (Athens: University of Georgia Press, 2000), 47.

47. "Bright Tobacco: An Old Negro the First to Cure It," *Progressive Farmer*, April 14, 1884, p. 4; Carter, "Cultural History Written with Lightning," in Rollins, *Hollywood as Historian*; for classic studies of the politics of the era, see Woodward, *Origins of the New South*; and V. O. Key, *Southern Politics in State and Nation* (New York: Vintage Books, 1949).

48. Hahn, *Making Tobacco Bright*, chapter 4.

49. Tatham, *Historical and Practical Essay*, 20–24; Thomas Singleton, *A Treatise on the Culture of Tobacco* (n.p., 1770?), 11–12, 20–23; Jennings, *Practical Treatise*, 39; Hahn, *Making Tobacco Bright*, 105–106, 110–114.

50. Siegel, *Roots of Southern Distinctiveness*, 62; Killebrew, "Report on the Culture and Curing," in *Tenth Census*, 3:583–880. While many twentieth-century sources referred to tobacco as a thirteen-month crop and while marketing might extend into the spring (especially for the landlord's portion of the crop), most of the crop sold in the fall immediately after harvest, and "some growers allow that the thirteenth [month] is put in during August and September when, for weeks, they spend their days priming in the fields, their nights watching the curing barns." See "Tobacco Comes to Town: Round the Year on the Market," in *Gamblers All!*, Folder 13, Box 14, Charles Horace Hamilton Papers, Special Collections Research Center, North Carolina State University, Raleigh, NC.

51. Killebrew, "Report on the Culture and Curing," in *Tenth Census*, 3:674–679; John S. Campbell, "The Perique Tobacco Industry of Louisiana," typescript, November 1971; and "The Perique Tobacco Industry of St. James Parish, La.: A World Monopoly," typescript, n.d., both in the John S. Campbell Papers, North Carolina State University.

Conclusion

1. National Cotton Council of America, "Cotton Ginnings," http://www .cotton.org/econ/cropinfo/ginnings.cfm; Lewis Cecil Gray, *History of Agriculture in the Southern United States to 1860*, 2 vols. (Washington, DC: Carnegie Institution of Washington, 1933) 2:692; John Hebron Moore, *The Emergence of the Cotton Kingdom in the Old Southwest, 1770–1860* (Baton Rouge: Louisiana State University Press, 1988), 286. I am indebted to John Gay and E. Phelps Gay of the E. J. Gay Planting and Manufacturing Co., Plaquemine, LA, for sharing their insights into modern sugar cane farming with me.

2. Gilbert Fite, *Cotton Fields No More: Southern Agriculture, 1865–1980* (Lexington: University Press of Kentucky, 1984); USDA/Agricultural Research Service, "Controlling Kudzu with Naturally Occurring Fungus," *Science Daily*, July 20, 2009, www.sciencedaily.com/releases/2009/07/090719185107.htm, accessed April 1, 2014; OECD / Food and Agriculture Organization of the United Nations, *OECD/ FAO Agricultural Outlook 2013* (OECD Publishing, 2013), 220–221.

3. Ulrich Bonnell Phillips, *Life and Labor in the Old South* (Boston: Little, Brown, 1929), 188. In describing slavery as nasty, brutish, and long lived, we are explicitly reframing Thomas Hobbes maxim that slavery was nasty, brutish, and short. On America's exceptional slave demographic experience, see Richard Follett, "The Demography of Slavery," in *The Routledge History of Slavery*, ed. Trevor Burnard and Gad Heuman (New York: Routledge, 2010), 119–137.

4. Nell Irvin Painter, "Miscegenation, Labor, and Power," in *The Evolution of Southern Culture*, ed. Numan V. Bartley (Athens: University of Georgia Press, 1985), 61–62; Jonathan M. Weiner, *The Social Origins of the New South: Alabama, 1860–1885* (Baton Rouge: Louisiana State University Press, 1978), 72–73, 184–85; Eric Hobsbawm, *The Age of Capital, 1848–1875* (New York: Charles Scribner, 1975), 154–155.

5. Alabama, "High Cotton," *Southern Star*, 1989 (writers: Scott Anders and Roger Murrah).

GUIDE TO FURTHER
READING

❧

The rise and fall of the plantation complex rightly occupies center stage in the history of the Americas. It was central to the rise and longevity of slavery and to what historian Barbara Solow has called "the Atlantic system." Slave grown commodities—produced on large estates for commercial export—were axiomatic to the growth of the New World and its incorporation into the international economy. The traffic in enslaved humans and the commodities they cultivated (sugar, tobacco, coffee, indigo, and rice above all) fueled the rapid expansion of the European economies during the eighteenth century and lay at the cornerstone of the transatlantic slave trade. The literature on slavery and the plantation revolution is large, but above all consult, Sidney Mintz, *Sweetness and Power: The Place of Sugar in Modern History* (1985); Barbara Solow, ed., *Slavery and the Rise of the Atlantic System* (1994); Philip Curtin, *The Rise and Fall of the Plantation Complex: Essays in Atlantic History* (1998); and Stuart B. Schwartz, ed., *Tropical Babylons: Sugar and the Making of the Atlantic World, 1450–1680* (2004).

The growth of slavery, however, was intrinsically linked with "the other foundational institution of modern imperial-capitalism, the plantation," Marcus Rediker argues. The spread of sugar production in the 1650s unleashed a voracious demand for enslaved labor and by the middle decades of the eighteenth century, the slave plantation had emerged, Robin Blackburn contends, "as the most distinctive product of European capitalism, colonialism, and maritime power." Key texts include Robin

Blackburn, *The Making of New World Slavery: From the Baroque to the Modern, 1492–1900* (1997, quote p. 350); David Brion Davis, *Inhuman Bondage: The Rise and Fall of Slavery in the New World* (2006); and Marcus Rediker, *The Slave Ship: A Human History* (2007, quote p. 43).

North American slaveholders swiftly embedded the plantation system and its corollary, racial slavery, into colonial American society. Tobacco plantations spread along the James and York Rivers, probing the Virginia Tidewater counties. A large literature on the growth of slavery and the plantation system in Virginia exists, though several key works offer class, racial, and economic explanations for the decline of servitude and rise of slavery in the Chesapeake: Edmund S. Morgan, *American Slavery—American Freedom: The Ordeal of Colonial Virginia* (1975); Winthrop Jordan, *White over Black: American Attitudes toward the Negro, 1550–1812* (1968); Allan Kulikoff, *Tobacco and Slaves: The Development of Southern Cultures in the Chesapeake, 1680–1800* (1986); and Anthony S. Parent Jr., *Foul Means: The Formation of a Slave Society in Virginia, 1660–1740* (2003). Two recent works on the dynamics of plantation life in Virginia, Maryland, and by contrast the British Caribbean merit particular attention: Lorena S. Walsh, *Motives of Honor, Pleasure and Profit: Plantation Management in the Colonial Chesapeake, 1607–1763* (2010); and Richard S. Dunn, *A Tale of Two Plantations: Slave Life and Labor in Jamaica and Virginia* (2014).

The growth of plantation slavery and the international market for rice receives attention in this book, but greater detail on South Carolina's early rice industry is available in Peter A. Coclanis, *The Shadow of a Dream: Economic Life and Death in the South Carolina Low Country, 1670–1920* (1989); S. Max Edelson, *Plantation Enterprise in Colonial South Carolina* (2006); and Peter A. Coclanis, "Distant Thunder: The Creation of a World Market in Rice and the Transformations It Wrought," *American Historical Review* 98 (October 1993): 1050–1078. The role of enslaved agriculturists in the development of the Carolina rice industry has received considerable attention, notably, Judith A. Carney, *Black Rice: The African Origins of Rice Cultivation in the Americas* (2001); and Carney and Richard Nicholas Rosomoff, *In the Shadow of Slavery: Africa's Botanical Legacy in the Atlantic World* (2009). Ecological matters are also detailed in Mart A. Stewart, *"What Nature Suffers to Groe": Life, Labor, and Landscape on the Georgia Coastal Plain, 1680–1920* (1996), which addresses, in part, the growth of the coastal Georgia rice industry. The definitive text on slave cultures in the eighteenth-century rice and tobacco belts is Philip D. Morgan, *Slave Counterpoint: Black Culture in the Eighteenth-Century Chesapeake and Low-country* (1998), though readers may also wish to consult Peter Wood, *Black Majority: Negroes in Colonial South Carolina from 1670 through the Stono Rebellion* (1974); Robert Olwell, *Masters, Slaves, and Subjects: The Culture of Power in the South Carolina Low Country, 1740–1790* (1998); and, for a magisterial overview of colonial slavery, Ira Berlin, *Many Thousands Gone: The First Two Centuries of Slavery in North America* (1998).

While colonial America largely turned on two slave-grown export crops (tobacco and rice), the agricultural history of the nineteenth-century South rested on the four main export commodities discussed in this volume: cotton, sugar, tobacco, and rice. These commodities were not grown exclusively, of course. Other staple products, notably hemp, were grown, but corn cultivation and livestock raising also occupied the slaves' time. So central was the plantation mode to life and labor in the Old South that the earliest histories of the region tended to focus attention on agricultural outputs and the work regimes associated with each crop. See, for instance, Ulrich Bonnell Phillips, *Life and Labor in the Old South* (1929); Lewis Cecil Gray, *History of Agriculture in the Southern United States to 1860* (2 vols., 1933); and Nöel Deerr, *The History of Sugar* (2 vols., 1949).

In the 1950s, however, several key historians reassessed the distinct plantation cultures. Central to this new thrust in history writing was the attention afforded to the enslaved. The best of these works was Kenneth M. Stampp, *The Peculiar Institution: Slavery in the Ante-Bellum South* (1956), which argued persuasively that plantations were "factories in the field" (p. 38). Nowhere was that analogy truer than in America's sugar cane district. In *Sugar Country: The Cane Sugar Industry in the South 1753–1950* (1953), J. Carlyle Sitterson explored the plantation system in south Louisiana's cane world. Sitterson's book set—and in many respects continues to define—scholarship on American sugar. As Richard Follett makes clear in this volume, sugar production was labor intensive and combined aspects of factory and farm on one site. Technically, the industry remained comparatively advanced, with major innovations in production occurring in the 1840s (with steam-powered sugar milling), although most planters did not adopt the more expensive vacuum processing techniques until the 1880s. On this important technical transformation, see John Heitmann, *The Modernization of the Louisiana Sugar Industry, 1830–1910* (1987).

For those interested in slavery and the pre–Civil War cane industry, Richard Follett, *The Sugar Masters: Planters and Slaves in Louisiana's Cane World, 1820–1860* (2005) provides the first modern, comprehensive history of the slave-based sugar complex in south Louisiana. He has also produced a major and freely available digital history project on US sugar with a fully searchable database and electronic resources on every sugar cane farmer in Louisiana from 1844 to 1917: www.sussex.ac.uk/louisianasugar (2008).

While Follett stresses the modern, capitalist, and ruthlessly exploitative world of sugar slavery, historians had been debating the nature of slavery and plantation capitalism in the cotton South from the 1970s. Although the so-called slavery debates raged most vociferously in the post–civil rights decades when Eugene D. Genovese, Robert Fogel, Stanley Engerman, Herbert Gutman, and others analyzed the nature and form of plantation slavery in the cotton South, today most scholars accept that the Old South featured premodern labor relations, albeit often on highly advanced and entrepreneurial plantations. See, for instance, Robert W. Fogel, *The Slavery Debates: A Retrospective, 1952–1990* (2003); and the still peerless *American Slavery* by Peter Kolchin (1993). In the past decade, scholars including Sven Beckert have argued forcefully that an era of "second slavery" existed and that the nineteenth-century slave plantation lay at the axis of America's economic development. Indeed, so central was the cotton complex to the rise of US capitalism that historians—including Edward Baptist—now contend that slave plantations ("slave labor camps" in Baptist's parlance) were emblematic of nineteenth-century modernization. See Sven Beckert, *Empire of Cotton: A New History of Global Capitalism* (2014); Walter Johnson, *Rivers of Dark Dreams: Slavery and Empire in the Cotton Kingdom* (2013); Edward E. Baptist, *The Half Has Never Been Told: Slavery and the Making of American Capitalism* (2014); Dale Tomich, *Through the Prism of Slavery: Labor, Control, and World Economy* (2004), and Seth Rockman and Sven Beckert eds., *Slavery's Capitalism: A New History of American Economic Development* (2016). Those seeking an introduction to the field of history and capitalism should look no further than Joyce Appleby's *The Relentless Revolution: A History of Capitalism* (2010).

This new direction in slavery studies, however, builds on a deep, complex literature that has explored in detail the economics of slavery and plantation agriculture. The most significant of these works are Dale Evans Swan, *The Structure and Profitability of the Antebellum Rice Industry* (1975);

Robert Fogel, *Without Consent or Contract: The Rise and Fall of American Slavery* (1989); Gavin Wright, *The Political Economy of the Cotton South: Households, Markets, and Wealth in the Nineteenth Century* (1978); Joyce E. Chaplin, *An Anxious Pursuit: Agricultural Innovation and Modernity in the Lower South, 1730–1815* (1993); and, more recently, Alan L. Olmstead and Paul W. Rhode, *Creating Abundance: Biological Innovation and American Agricultural Development* (2008). Scholars who have focused on the expansionist and westward thrust of the cotton regime include Adam Rothman, *Slave Country: American Expansion and the Origins of the Deep South* (2005); and Watson W. Jennison, *Cultivating Race: The Expansion of Slavery in Georgia, 1750–1860* (2012); while the nature of cotton trading receives attention in Harold D. Woodman, *King Cotton and His Retainers: Financing and Marketing the Cotton Crop of the South, 1800–1925* (1968); Scott P. Marler, *The Merchants' Capital: New Orleans and the Political Economy of the Nineteenth Century South* (2013); and Bruce E. Baker and Barbara Hahn, *The Cotton Kings: Capitalism and Corruption in Turn of the Century New York and New Orleans* (2015). Brian Schoen addresses the place of cotton within sectional thinking prior to the Civil War in *The Fragile Fabric of Union: Cotton, Federal Politics, and the Global Origins of the Civil War* (2010) while Giorgio Riello—like Sven Beckert—adopts a global, transnational approach to the growth of worldwide cotton markets in *Cotton: The Fabric That Made the World* (2015).

Slave emancipation and military defeat in the Civil War transformed the plantation system and rendered null the forced dominion of slavery. Key works on the monumental shift in labor and social relations include, but are not limited to, Julie Saville, *The Work of Reconstruction: From Slave to Wage Laborer in South Carolina, 1860–1880* (1994); Susan E. O'Donovan, *Becoming Free in the Cotton South* (2007); Joseph P. Reidy, *From Slavery to Agrarian Capitalism in the Cotton Plantation South: Central Georgia, 1800–1880* (1992); John C. Rodrigue, *Reconstruction in the Cane Fields: From Slavery to Free Labor in Louisiana's Sugar Parishes, 1862–1880* (2001); and Rebecca J. Scott, *Degrees of Freedom: Louisiana and Cuba after Slavery* (2005). Scholarly works focusing on the ways that former slaveholders attempted (often in vain) to maintain a firm grip over plantation agriculture and African American workers include Richard Follett, Eric Foner, and Walter Johnson, *Slavery's Ghost: The Problem of Freedom in the Age of Emancipation* (2011); Thavolia Glymph, *Out of the House of Bondage: The Transformation of the Plantation Household* (2008); and Stephen Kantrowitz, *Ben Tillman & the Reconstruction of White Supremacy* (2000). Powerful accounts of life as an African American cotton worker in the years following slavery are given in two indispensable texts: Leon F. Litwack, *Trouble in Mind: Black Southerners in the Age of Jim Crow* (1998); and Steven Hahn, *A Nation under Our Feet: Black Political Struggles in the Rural South from Slavery to the Great Migration* (2003).

While cotton, rice, and sugar (and their attendant labor regimes) have often occupied center stage in histories of the plantation South, tobacco cultivation continued apace during the nineteenth century and enjoyed revitalization once new crop varietals were developed and tobacco cultivation extended to Kentucky. Key works include Barbara Hahn, *Making Tobacco Bright: Creating an American Commodity, 1617–1937* (2011); Jeffrey R. Kerr-Ritchie, *Freedpeople in the Tobacco South: Virginia, 1860–1990* (1999); Christopher Waldrep, *Night Riders: Defending Community in the Black Patch, 1880–1915* (1993); and Tracy Campbell, *The Politics of Despair: Power and Resistance in the Tobacco Wars* (1993).

As Peter Coclanis makes clear in the first chapter of this book, US rice farmers faced commodity hell by the late nineteenth century. Like other plantation crop cultivators in the American South, rice farmers simply could not compete in increasingly global, competitive markets. Important works that assess the economic and social transformations associated with sharecropping, tenancy, international marketing, and competition within a global marketplace in further detail include Gilbert Fite, *Cotton Fields No More: Southern Agriculture, 1865–1980* (1984); Pete Daniel, *Breaking the Land: The Transformation of Cotton, Tobacco, and Rice Cultures since 1880* (1985); and John B. Rehder, *Delta Sugar: Louisiana's Vanishing Landscape* (1999).

This short book brings together the history of America's agricultural commodities and explains the rise and fall of the Southern plantation complex. As the authors make clear, global market opportunities were the midwife at the South's economic birth in the eighteenth century; 150 years later, international competition humbled many Southern staple farmers. Those who endured the onslaught of global competition survived through innovation and mechanization, by shifting from labor-intensive agriculture to capital-intensive agriculture, and by exploiting agricultural workers on "neoplantations" owned by corporate conglomerates. These issues are ably examined by Jeannie Whayne, *Delta Empire: Lee Wilson and the Transformation of Agriculture in the New South* (2011); Cindy Hahamovitch, *No Man's Land: Jamaican Guestworkers in America and the Global History of Deportable Labor* (2011); and Mae M. Ngai, *Impossible Subjects: Illegal Aliens and the Making of Modern America* (2004). Whether bossing a Jamaican cane worker in Florida or dragooning immigrant workers on a Texas cotton farm, however, forced labor has remained a persistent and almost unbroken thread to staple farming; it defined America's plantation kingdom in the past and, sadly, continues to shape its present.

INDEX

Page numbers in *italics* indicate figures.

Africa: ginning technology in, 109; rice technology in, 4, 15; tobacco exports to, 106, 111, 117–18
agrarian radicalism, 111–13
Alabama, 119–20
alcoholic beverages, distilled, and rice, 26
American Cotton Planter, 49, 54
American South. *See* South
American Sugar Refining Company, 83
American Tobacco Company, 108–9, 111
Anne Arundel County, Maryland, 20
"anticommodity" line, 35
Arab Agricultural Revolution, 24
"articulation of production modes" approach, 35
Asia: cotton from, 32–33; European trade with, 32, 33; ginning technology in, 109; kudzu from, 120; rice and, 13, 15, 25, 120; sugar from, 32–33
"Atlantic system," 151

Bailyn Bernard, 30, 36
Banks, Nathaniel, 77
Baton Rouge, Louisiana, 71
Beckert, Sven, 105, 154

Belich, James, 62
Bergad, Laird, 84
Blackburn, Robin, 151
Black Patch Wars, 111–13
Bonsack cigarette-rolling machine, 108
Boré, Étienne de, 65, 87
Branch, Thomas, 104
brands of tobacco, 104–5
Bright Flue-Cured Cigarette Tobacco, 91, 113–17
Britain: cotton in, 40–41, 42; Navigation Acts in, 101–2, 103; tobacco imports in, 102–3
burley tobacco, 110–11
Burling, Walter, 53
"buy environment," 26

Cail, Jean-François, 73
Cantillon, Richard, 17
capital, allocation of, 52–55
capitalism: in Europe, 29–30; industrialization, cotton farming, and, 40; mercantilism, 101; plantation type of, 154; shift from merchant to industrial type of, 62. *See also* global capitalism

Carter, Landon, 104
ceteris paribus, 27
Charleston, South Carolina, 4, 20
Chesapeake system of tobacco cultivation, 97, 100–101
China, recruitment of labor from, 77–78
Chinese Exclusion Act of 1882, 80
cigarette industry, 8, 108–9, 118
Civil War: cotton and, 39, 55–57; economy after, 121; Louisiana after, 76–77; political conflicts preceding, 54–55; raw-materials crisis of, 55; sugar industry after, 76–80, 89; tobacco and, 107–10, 116. *See also* slave emancipation
Claiborne, W. C. C., 66
Cole, Arthur, 33
Collot, Georges, 65
colonial regulation of tobacco, 95–98
Columbian exchange and rice, 15
commercial relationships and tobacco, 94–95
commodities, 12–13. *See also* export commodities
commodity hell: overview of, 5, 13, 92; rice and, 37–38; sugar and, 63, 83, 90; tobacco and, 92, 113
competition in markets: for cotton, 57; current, 119; for export commodities, 3, 5–6; history of, 120–21; logic of, 53–54; South and, 121–22; for sugar, 6, 9–10, 81–83
Connecticut Shade-Grown tobacco, 91
consumption: of cotton, 40–41; of rice, 13–15; of sugar, 14, 68
cotton: agronomists and, 47–48; from Asia, 32–33; after Civil War, 55–57; consumption of, 40–41; continental consolidation of, 46–52, 47; demand for, 14, 44–46; expansion of production of, 46–50, 47; as export, 40; free small farmers and, 50; harvesting, 41–42, 44–45, 49–50; as "hashish of West," 41; history of, 42–46; hybrids of, 53; in India, 3; market for, 4–5, 40–42, 57; mechanization and, 43;

modern production of, 119–20; rice, competition with, 32; slavery and, 44, 46, 49–51, 52–55; Southern production of, 1, 7, 29–40; supply of, 44–46, 55; switch to cane farming from, 70–71; transportation costs and, 49; upland species of, 47; in Yazoo-Mississippi Delta, 51–52. *See also* cotton textiles
cotton gin, 5, 39, 45, 109
cotton manufacturing, 57–60
cotton textiles, 41–42, 44, 57–59
crops: as commodities, 12; staple, and slavery, 1–2. *See also* cotton; rice; sugar; tobacco
Cuba: Chinese laborers in, 78; fall of plantation structure in, 84, 85; plantation system, 33, 64; slave emancipation in, 86; sugar exported by, 75, 81, 82
Cuban-Seed Cigar Leaf tobacco, 91
cultivation: of rice, 15–20, 24–25; of tobacco, 91, 93–94, 97, 98–101, 116, 156
Cunnington, E. H., 88
curing tobacco, 97, 114, 116

Danson, J. T., 46
Darby, William, 67
Dark Fire-Cured Tobacco, 111, 112, 116–18
De Bow's Review, 49
Decker, Michael, 24
demand: for cotton, 14, 44–46; for cotton textiles, 42; for rice, 24–30; for sugar, 14, 68–69; for tobacco, 14, 102. *See also* price and demand
Demopolis, Alabama, 119–20
Derosne, Louis-Charles, 73
Doar, David, 36–37
Duncan, Stephen, 52

Eastern Dark Fire-Cured Tobacco, 91
economy of South, 5, 55, 59–60, 121, 156–57. *See also* markets; profits; wealth
emancipation. *See* slave emancipation
entrepreneurship: agricultural, 38; rice industry and, 16–17

Europe: capital from, 52–55; capitalist economy of, 29–30; cotton and, 41, 42, 43–44; cultivation of rice in, 24–25; demand for rice in, 25–26, 28, 29; demand for tobacco in, 102; raw-materials crisis in, 55; sugar beets in, 63, 82–83; sugar in, 3; trade with Asia, 32, 33

export commodities: centrality of, to Southern experience, 1–2; competitive market for, 3, 5–6; global movement of, 4; slavery and, 153; transformation of South and, 7–8. *See also* cotton; rice; sugar; tobacco

factory, invention of, 41
Farmers' Alliance, 115
Fite, Gilbert, 120
Fitzhugh, Henry, 104
Florida: acquisition of, 48; cane farming in, 69; rice cultivation in, 18, 19; sugar factories in, 88–89
France, government tobacco monopoly in, 99
fungible goods, 12–13

Galloway, J. R., 64
gang labor on sugar plantations, 74, 77, 78, 80, 85
Gayarré, Charles, 65
Genovese's law, 144n15
Georgia: rice cultivation in, 19; slavery in, 21
"ghost acres," 29, 43
Giffen goods, 26–27
global capitalism: rice in expansion and elaboration of, 15; slavery, sugar, and, 61; South as laboratory of, 59–60
global networks of cotton, 42–46
Gray, Lewis Cecil, 91, 99

Haiti, sugar production on, 65
Hammond, James Henry, 1, 39, 121
harvesting: cotton, 41–42, 44–45, 49–50; sugar cane, 74; tobacco, 97, 99, 100–101, 116

Haskell, Thomas, 26
Hawaii, sugar from, 9, 63, 81, 82
Helm, Elijah, 58
heritability, scientists of, 142n2
Heyward, Nathaniel, 22
Hobsbawm, Eric, 121
hogsheads: of sugar, 71; of tobacco, 96
Holmes, Andrew, 37–38
Holt, Thomas, 77
"humanitarian sensibility" and demand for rice, 26
Hunt's Merchants Magazine, 68

iatrogenesis and rice industry, 16
imports: of rice, 33; of sugar, 75–76
indentured labor and sugar production, 79–80
India: cotton in, 42, 43; cotton textiles from, 44; rice from, 32
indigo, 32–33
industrialization: cotton farming and, 40, 41; cotton manufacturing and, 57–60; of sugar plantations, 72–74; tobacco and, 103–5
Industrial Revolution, 41, 60
International Cotton Exposition of 1881, 57–58

Jamaica, postemancipation sugar industry in, 77
Jones, Alice Hanson, 20

Kentucky: Black Patch Wars in, 111–13; tobacco cultivation and manufacturing in, 105–8; White Burley Tobacco from, 110–11
kudzu, 120

labor: in Chesapeake system of tobacco cultivation, 100–101; compatibility of technology with, 73; as constraining cotton production, 55–56; for cotton growing and harvesting, 41–42, 44–45, 49–50, 55–57; global movement of, 4;

labor (*continued*)
indentured, 79–80; for sugar production, 62, 77–80; for textile factories, 41–42, 58–59; for tobacco production, 112. *See also* slavery
latent historical events, 30, 36
Locke, John, 12
Louisiana: Baton Rouge, 71; cane farming in, 69; centralized production in, 86; after Civil War, 76–77; constraints on sugar production in, 69–70; cotton in, 6; decline of sugar industry in, 88; expansion of sugar production in, 66–67, 70–72; immigrant labor in, 78; New Orleans, 6, 49, 68, 105–6; origins of sugar production in, 65–66; recovery of sugar industry in, 81, 82; slavery in, 66, 67–68, 72; steam-powered mills in, 72–73; St. James Parish, 66, 67, 117; as sugar colony, 9–10, 61, 64; tobacco in, 99, 117, 118. *See also* Louisiana Sugar Planters Association
Louisiana Purchase, 48, 66
Louisiana Sugar Bowl, 77–78
Louisiana Sugar Planters Association (LSPA), 78–79, 80, 86, 87
low country of South Carolina, 17–18, 37

MacPherson, David, 32
manifest historical events, 30
markets: competitive logic of, 53–54; for cotton, 4–5, 40–42; for cotton textiles, 44; global, and economic birth of South, 156–57; institutional relations with, 117; regulation of, 98, 117–18; for rice, 25–29, 33–35; for slaves, 68; for sugar, 6, 9–10, 63–64, 67, 68–69, 75, 81–83; for tobacco, 94–95, 101–3. *See also* competition in markets; tariff protection for sugar
Marshall, Alfred, 26–27
Martin, Bonnie, 53
Marx, Karl: on commodities, 13; on slavery, 17; on "windfalls," 35
Maryland, wealth in, 20

McKinley Tariff, 87
mercantilism, 101
Merivale, Herman, 46
Mitchell, Timothy, 56
mosquito-borne diseases, 19
Myint, Hla, 35
myths of Dixie, 1–2, 122
myths of origin: of bright tobacco, 114–15; of technologies, 109–10; of tobacco type, 113

Native Americans: land of, 48, 51; tobacco and, 99
Naturalization Act of 1870, 79–80
Navigation Acts of England, 101–2, 103
New Orleans: cotton receipts in, 6, 49; slave markets in, 68; tobacco and, 105–6
New South mythmaking, 109–10, 114–15
North, textile industrialization of, 105
North Carolina, rice cultivation in, 18, 19

Old Southwest, rice industry in, 38
Oryza glaberrima, 15
Oryza sativa, 15
Otaheite cane, 69
Ottoman Empire, 44

Patout, Mary Ann, 87
Perique Tobacco, 117, 118
Philippine sugar, 81, 120
Phillips, Ulrich, B., 120
plantation complex, 6–7, 11, 57, 70, 89, 119, 151. *See also* plantation revolution; plantation system
Plantation Illusion, 109–10, 114–15
plantation kingdom: fall of, 84–90; legacies of, 119–22. *See also* planter class; slavery
plantation revolution, 7, 66–67, 72, 74
plantation system, 9–10, 61–65, 77–78, 84–85, 90, 122
planter class: central factories and, 85–86; cotton and, 46, 51–52, 53, 57; sugar and, 66, 71, 76, 78–79, 80–81
Polk, James K., 71

Pomeranz, Kenneth, 43

Porter, Alexander, 76

price and demand: in Black Patch Wars, 111–13; for cotton, 48; for rice, 26–28, 36–37; for sugar, 68; for tobacco, 95, 101

priming method of harvesting tobacco, 116

profits: from cotton, 42; from rice, 20–21, 22–23; from sugar, 67, 76; from tobacco, 20. *See also* wealth

Progressive Farmer, 115

Puerto Rico, sugar industry in, 32, 64, 85, 89

quality of tobacco, 96–98

race and Black Patch Wars, 111–12, 113

Ramsey, James, 74

ratoons, 96, 100

Reconstruction, 56, 79

Rediker, Marcus, 151

re-exporting tobacco, 101–2, 103

regulation: of markets, 98, 117–18; of tobacco, 95–98

ribbon cane, 69–70, 73

rice: Asia and, 13, 15, 25, 120; commodity hell for, 37–38; competitive advantages of South as supplier of, 31; consumption of, 13–15; convergence of "causal registers" for, 32; cotton, competition with, 32; cultivation of, 15–20, 24–25; demand for and supply of, 24–30; elite growers of, 20–23; as export commodity, 16–17, 33; as Giffen good, 26–27; market for, 33–35; markets for, 25–29; in Old Southwest, 38; quality of, 36–37; resources on, 152–53; roads to perdition for, 30–37; slavery and, 19–20; Southeast Asia and, 3, 32–33, 35; sunk costs and, 34; supply of, 28–29, 32–33, 35–36. *See also* tidal rice zone

Richardson, Francis DuBose, 67

Rillieux, Norbert, 73

Rolfe, John, 92–93

rural cultivators and cotton, 56–57

Saint-Domingue: slave rebellion on, 45, 51, 54, 65; sugar production on, 64–65

Saint-Méry, Moreau de, 64–65

Scarborough, William K., 22

"second slavery," 7, 74–75, 154

Selznick, David O., 2

sharecropping: cotton and, 57, 59; overview of, 10, 121; sugar and, 62, 77, 85; tobacco and, 92, 94, 116–17

Slade, Elisha, 114, 115

slave emancipation: consequences of, 76, 155–56; cotton and, 5, 55–56; credit relations and, 115–16; loss of wealth through, 37, 76; political economy of, 116; sugar cane and, 9, 56; tobacco and, 93–94, 108, 110–17

slave revolts: in Louisiana, 66; on Saint-Domingue, 45, 51, 54, 65

slavery: colonial, 153; as compatible with modernity, 75, 112; cotton growing and, 44, 46, 49–51; as distinguishing Old South from rest of country, 2–3; economics of, 154–55; gang labor on sugar plantations, 74, 77, 78, 80, 85; investment in, 6–7; justification for, 54; in Louisiana, 66, 67–68, 72; plantation complex and, 151–52; reinforcement of institution of, 50; rice cultivation and, 16, 19–20, 22–23; scholarly consensus on, 6, 154; in South Carolina, 4, 21, 22–23; staple crops and, 1–2; sugar production and, 61, 67–68, 72, 154; tobacco cultivation and, 100–101; tragedy of, 120–21. *See also* slave emancipation; slaves

slavery debates, 6, 154

slaves: as commodities, 12; loans secured by mortgages on, 52–53; rice plantations as platforms for raising and selling of, 34; year-round employment of, 112, 144n15

Solow, Barbara, 151

South: competitive advantages of, for cotton, 46–52; competitive advantages of, for rice, 31; economy of, 5, 55, 59–60, 121,

South (*continued*)
156–57; in history of cotton, 44, 45–46; as laboratory of global capitalism, 59–60; transformation of, 7, 39–40. *See also specific states*

South Carolina: Charleston, 4, 20; low country of, 17–18, 37; origins of rice cultivation in, 16–17; slavery in, 4, 21, 22–23; St. Johns Berkeley Parish, 29; wealth in, 20–21. *See also tidal rice zone*

Southeast Asia, rice from, 3, 32–33, 35

Spanish colonies, tobacco in, 99–100

spinning jenny, 43, 109

spinning mule, 43

steam-powered sugar mills, 72–73

stemming tobacco, 106

Stephen (slave) and bright tobacco, 114–15

"stint laws," 96

St. James Parish, Louisiana, 66, 67, 117

St. Johns Berkeley Parish, South Carolina, 29

strike action in sugar industry, 78, 79

Stubbs, William C., 88

sugar: from Asia, 32–33; centralization of milling of, 84–86; after Civil War, 76–77, 89; commodity hell for, 63, 83, 90; constraints on production of, 69–70; consumption of, 14, 68; demand for, 14, 68–69; in Europe, 3; expansion of production of, 63, 66–67, 70–72; fall of plantation order and, 84–90; federal protection for, 8–9, 66–67, 70, 71, 76, 83, 88; global production of, 81–82; harvesting and processing of, 74; history of, 61–62; imports of, 75–76; labor for production of, 77–80; markets for, 6, 9–10, 63–64, 67, 68–69, 75, 81–83; origins of Louisiana production of, 65–66; plantation mode of production of, 62–64, 89; power relations and, 80–81; research and experiment stations, 87–88; Saint-Domingue and, 64–65; slavery and, 61,

67–68, 72, 154; technological improvements for, 72–73, 80, 86–87

sugar beets: European, 63, 82–83; US, 83

supply: of cotton, 44–46, 55; of rice, 28–29, 32–33, 35–36

swamps, irrigated and tidal, for rice cultivation, 17–18

Swan, Dale E., 23

tariff protection for sugar, 8–9, 66–67, 70, 71, 76, 83, 88

technology: for bright tobacco, 115–16; for cultivation of tobacco, 93–94; human action as shaping, 98; for manufacturing of tobacco, 108–9; modern production, 119–20; for sugar production, 72–73, 80, 86–87, 153. *See also cotton gin*

tenant farming: cotton and, 57, 59; overview of, 121; sugar and, 62–63, 85, 88

Texas: annexation of, 48; cane farming in, 69; sugar factories in, 88

Thibodaux Massacre, 79

tidal rice zone: agricultural units in, 29; fertility of, 31–32; geographical limitations of, 31; morbidity and mortality in, 19; profits in, 20–21, 22–23; size and location of, 17–19

tobacco: Black Patch Wars, 111–13; Bright Flue-Cured, 91, 113–17; burley, 110–11; Civil War and, 107–10; colonial regulation of, 95–98; commercial relationships and, 94–95; commodification of, 92, 113; commodity hell for, 92, 113; cultivation of, 91, 93–94, 97, 98–101, 116, 156; curing, 97, 114, 116; decline in production of, 50; demand for, 14, 102; distinctions between "shipping" and "manufacturing," 103–5; farming of, after Civil War, 116; harvesting, 97, 99, 100–101, 116; industrialization and, 103–5; in Kentucky, 105–8; market economy in, 7–8; markets for, 94–95, 101–3; Perique, 117; postbellum warehouses for, 116–17; profits in, 20;

quality of, 96–98; ratoons, 96, 100; re-exporting of, 101–2, 103; stemming, 106; taxes on, 108; varietal types, 91–95, 109–10, 117–18; westward expansion of production of, 105–7; White Burley, 110–11

tobacco manufacturing, 103–4, 106–8

Tomich, Dale, 74

transatlantic trade: in cotton, 52; in sugar, slaves, and goods, 61; in tobacco, 107

transportation infrastructure in South, 16, 28, 31, 49, 52, 70

tropical sugar producers, 61–64

United States Sugar Corporation, 88–89

US Department of Agriculture (USDA), 91, 94, 108, 117, 118

vacuum processing facilities for sugar, 73, 86

varietal types of tobacco, 91–95, 109–10, 117–18

"vent-for-surplus" line, 35–36

Virginia: regulation of tobacco in, 96; slavery and plantation system in, 152; tobacco grown in, 95–96, 107–8; tobacco manufacturing in, 104

Virginia Company, 25

wages in cotton manufacturing, 59

Walker tariff, 71

Warren, Robert Penn, 111–12

water frame, 43, 45

Watson, Andrew, 24

wealth: in Anne Arundel County, Maryland, 20; of cotton farmers, 22; distributions of, 21–22; of free population, 68; in global cotton trade, 40; loss of, through slave emancipation, 37, 76; in Louisiana, 66; of rice planters, 20–21, 22–23; of sugar cane planters, 22; in Yazoo-Mississippi Delta, 52

Western Dark Fire-Cured Tobacco, 91

westward expansion and tobacco cultivation, 105–7

White Burley Tobacco, 110–11

Whitney, Eli, 45, 109

Whittier, John Greenleaf, 41

Yazoo-Mississippi Delta, 51–52